The Way It Was
The North Dakota Frontier Experience
Book Two: Norwegian Homesteaders

Published in the Series

The Way It Was:
The North Dakota Frontier Experience

Book One: The Sod-busters, 1996

Book Two: Norwegian Homesteaders, 1998

Book Three: The Cowboys & Ranchers, 1999

Book Four: Germans from Russia Settlers, 1999

Coming in 2002

Book Five: The Native People

Book Six: The Townspeople

The Way It Was

The North Dakota Frontier Experience
Book Two:

Norwegian Homesteaders

Everett C. Albers and D. Jerome Tweton, Editors

THE GRASS ROOTS PRESS
Fessenden, North Dakota 58438
Second Edition, 2001

This book is dedicated to Denny Tweton,
  the leader of the Oregon Tweton clan.
The series is dedicated to the memory of North Dakota pioneers.

Editors: *Everett C. Albers and D. Jerome Tweton*
Designer: *Otto Design of Bismarck, ND*

© 2001 by The Grass Roots Press

PO Box 407
Fessenden, North Dakota 58438-0407

Published by The Grass Roots Press

Printed in Canada

10 9 8 7 6 5 4 3 2

International Standard Book Number: 0-9650778-2-9 (Book 2)
International Standard Book Number: 0-9650778-1-0 (6-Volume Set)

Library of Congress Catalog Card Number: 98-89183

Table of Contents

Acknowledgments

*T*HE PHOTOGRAPHS IN THIS COLLECTION come from one of North Dakota's greatest resources, The Fred Hultstrand History in Pictures Collection, North Dakota Institute for Regional Studies, North Dakota State University, Fargo. Over 900 photographs from the Institute's collection are on the Library of Congress American Memory web site because of a Library of Congress/ Ameritech National Digital Library Award. All captions are those noted in the collection. The cover photograph is identified as "Log-sod house, Herman Lien, Adams, North Dakota, 1890." The Grass Roots Press gratefully acknowledges the ongoing support of John Bye and the North Dakota Institute for Regional Studies.

The editors also thank the staff of the State Historical Society of North Dakota, the home of 5,000 stories of North Dakota pioneers from which we gleaned these sixteen.

And we thank our wives, Leslie Albers and Paula Tweton. Just as few of the Norwegian men who came to Dakota could not have survived without the tireless work and sacrifice of the women who did most of the work, we would never get a book to press without Leslie's and Paula's weeks of proofreading, insistent encouragement, and sound advice. In fact, any mistakes in this book are likely a result of our failure to take their advice.

About the editing . . .

The words are those of the Norwegian homesteaders. We changed the stories recorded in the third-person by WPA workers to first-person narratives. We also made some punctuation and grammatical changes and occasionally inserted words for clarity.

Norwegian Storytellers

Everett C. Albers

The Norwegian homesteaders certainly had the right stuff to make it in Dakota.

They survived, and many thrived, on what was sometimes a less-than-hospitable land because of their frugal, make-do approach to living in Dakota. In the words of Anders Elken, "I never spent any money. Every penny I made was used for things I needed."

THEY CAME FROM THE MOUNTAINS and sea-shores of Norway to nearly every part of North Dakota. They came for the land and the promise of better times. Dakota was often less than they hoped.

The sixteen stories in this collection include Norwegian settlers to the four corners of the state. Ole Sims came to Ambrose in the northwest to work on the railroad and stayed to homestead in Divide County in 1903 in what he first thought was a "country desolate and dreary," which "appeared unfit for civilization." The problem the following year was too much water. Ole says he "would have left . . . if I had not already invested so much money. I decided to make the best of the matter." Mikkel Hylden took his wife and three children north of Grand Forks, around Grafton, in the northeast, in 1881. Since the land was yet to be surveyed, he plowed halfway into the wrong quarter-section. He managed the first year by planting a garden a mile from his shack. Hanna Paulson joined her husband at Ft. Abercrombie in the southwest in 1876 before the railroad got there. She lived in a tent and shared her vegetables with an old Indian woman, a dispossessed traveler who had even less than she did. Down in southwestern North Dakota, Louise Woodwick La Mont "was so homesick, I couldn't even cry." She remembers living on the thinnest of pancakes made with a bit of flour for three days while her husband was gone in a blizzard. She didn't have much, but what she had, she shared with her only companion, her dog.

To make it in Dakota, the Norwegian homesteaders had to make do. They bought only what was necessary, for the most part. Anders Elken, homesteader in Wells County, recalled that, "Whenever time permitted during the summer, the first couple of years, I would pick buffalo bones and haul them to town where I received $8.00 to $11.00 per ton. This brought some ready cash for incidental expenses — not to spend, for I never spent any money. Every penny I made was used for things I needed." Some brought spinning wheels with them from the old country, others made them. Most of the earliest immigrants made all of their own clothing, from scratch — from the wool of sheep grazing on the virgin prairie. They made candles from the tallow of animals they butchered, beer from barley and hops they planted in land they broke with oxen, soap with wood ash from the trees they felled. They even made clocks from wood. To say the Norwegian homesteaders were frugal is almost an understatement. They made do. John E. Bagstad, who came to the Kaldor settlement on the Goose River near what is now Hillsboro concludes, "Our requirements were not so very great — a few sacks of flour for the winter, some green coffee, salt, sugar, syrup, dried apples and some spices — and we were all set for a six-month winter."

They did borrow money on occasion, often remembered by those who did as a bad decision. Two reported losing land because of a mortgage. Louis Froguer says that being turned down for a loan was the best luck he had. "I have been thankful many times that I couldn't make a loan as I might have been tempted to do as the others had done [borrow and not be able to pay back]. Eighteen ninety-one was the beginning of my good times."

The good times did not stay, but there were enough to sustain those who had adapted to a country where more often than not there was too much or too little water, too many grasshoppers and gophers, and hail storms just before harvest. Then there was the early snow before harvest could be done. Homesteader Thomas Alstad could not harvest in 1882, so he was left without seed to plant the next spring in the new ground he had broken, and no money to buy any. Alstad ingeniously poured water on the floor of an unused shack down by the river and used the smooth surface to flail out enough grain to plant. He found a way to separate the wheat from the chaff.

Interviewed about forty years after their homesteading experience, the Norwegian pioneers in Dakota often cited the exact price they got for their grain and what they paid for necessities. They talked about their schools, churches, and their neighbors. They remembered some good times — dances, community gatherings on the Fourth of July, and getting the *Decorah Posten* in the mail and enjoying reading the news in the Norwegian language.

Their words were recorded and often reported in the third-person with varying degrees of interpretation and embellishment by those doing the interviewing. In a sense, what follows in the sixteen stories in this collection are an edited interpretation sixty years after someone else edited and interpreted the stories of what early pioneers remembered about the way it was forty to sixty years before. Yet, in spite of being removed by as much as twelve decades from those times and twice filtered, the Norwegian homesteaders give us a sense of what it must have been like. More interestingly, their essential humanity, and each of their special stories, comes through. In each of the chapters, there is a sentence or two which tells a compelling tale and leaves the reader wishing they could ask for more.

Thomas Alstad says simply, "It took me years to get over that." His seventeen year old son was killed by lightning as he stood next to him in the store he built after losing his farm when the grain froze before harvest in August several years before.

Hans Amble started farming in 1888. He says, "The first year we harvested a good crop was in 1905." Before that, there was total failure from drought, frost, and gophers. But he talks about building a school and church the first year the crop comes in.

Peter B. Anderson tells how he got up early in the morning to set off for a neighboring farm to visit. The ten-mile trip took all day — ". . . the oxen were very slow walkers, and there would be little time left for visiting."

Nels Arntzen was caught in a blizzard on a trip to the river for wood with his brother-in-law in 1882-83. Nels says, "Our greatest difficulty was keeping awake, for I am sure if we had gone to sleep, we would have frozen to death. I had to fight with my brother-in-law all night to keep him awake."

John E. Bagstad went to school in the first years of the 1880s in a one-room school where the new Americans learned geography by reciting in unison the names of the states, their capitals, main rivers, and main cities. Then students turned their backs to the map and recited from memory. Says Bagstad, "We learned a whole lot about the United States of America in this fashion." Bagstad also recalled the homemade blackboard and the make-do eraser — the hind leg of a jack rabbit.

Getting to Dakota was no easy task. Halvor and his wife Brita Berg brought their family to Dakota in 1873, among the earliest of immigrants in search of land. His son Nicolai says, in typical laconic understatement, "Mother saw her share of hardship on this journey." She walked behind the livestock, baked, washed clothes, milked the cows. Once on the banks of the Goose River, she carried water from the river, which they had to soften with soap they made from wood ashes. Her hands were so sore from this make-do soap that they never healed between washings.

Kari Berg Brenna and husband Ole came to a homestead between Grand Forks and Northwood in the late 1870s. She "had to make all of the clothing, even the underwear. . . . I did not have a spinning wheel at first." She solved her problem by bartering her sewing for spinning with a neighbor.

Lured by reports of a land of opportunity, Anders Elken squatted until he was old enough to file on land in Wells County. He is the one who "never spent any money." After years of working on his parents' farm, he "batched" on his claim from 1896 until 1901, "doing my own cooking, dish washing, clothes washing and housekeeping." He married, perhaps as much of necessity as love, when the work became too much for him. Few of the men interviewed recalled "batching" with any fondness.

Louis Froguer changed his name from Larson to his uncle's when he became a citizen — it just saved time and trouble — he was brought to America by the uncle and lived with him before homesteading. He only harvested part of his crop in 1891, what he called "the beginning of the good times," because it snowed on October 25. The snow did not leave until April 1892. He got $1.00 per bushel for what he harvested before the snow, but only 30 cents for what he finally threshed in June 1892 because it was of such a poor grade after sitting for eight months. Yet it was far better than the years of total failure before 1891.

Albert Hoiland went on to selling windmills and machinery and inventing improved farm implements after his experience on his parents' homestead in Barnes County. He offers detailed instructions on making soap, candles, and beer. He observes, "Mother was a frugal woman who made as many of the household necessities in her own home as she could, including soap." An entrepreneurial youngster, he went south to LaMoure County at age twelve to trap gophers and made $30. Then he trapped muskrat, mink, a few raccoons, and a single otter. That netted him $100 — enough to buy himself a suit and one for his older brother John, which he remembers cost $35. In fact, Albert remembers exactly how many animals of each kind he trapped.

The most detailed story in the collection is told by Mikkel Hylden, who decided to raft his belongings from Grand Forks down river to his homestead near Minto. He and his companion try without much success to get something to eat, nearly capsize, and suffer an evening with the bane of the early Red River Valley settlers' lives, the mosquito. Either Hylden or his interviewer interjected attempts at humor into his story: " . . . we received the unwelcome company in the form of swarms of mosquitoes bent on taking unfair advantage of us. Well, the upshot of the whole matter was that we had to take turns smoking the pipe of peace in order to keep the pests quiet and likewise take turns catching a few winks of sleep."

Of her long nights alone in the shack in Adams County while her husband hauled lumber from Richardton to Haynes — a trip which took a week or more — Louise Woodward La Mont (she married a Frenchman) says, "It was surely trying. Coyotes would howl around our shack at night and scare me nearly to death." But in spite of fires, ill-

Harmony in the home, in more ways than one . . .
Two women are seated with quilts on their laps, a sewing machine with a metal foot pedal between them, and a man standing behind them holding a guitar. From left to right they are Marie Gjevre, Ole I. Gjevre, and Kari Erickson. There is a bookcase behind Marie Gjevre. Fairdale, North Dakota, 189-?.

ness, and loneliness, Louise says, ". . . we were there on the homestead; we made up our minds we would stick it out."

Future North Dakota Governor Ragnvold A. Nestos "came to Buxton with little or no work to be had because the President Grover Cleveland hard times. The Fourth of July was celebrated in that town that year, but I had a lone nickel with which to celebrate the day." Nestos found a mentor who made it possible for him to earn a law degree and become an orator and debater much in demand on Fourth of July celebrations throughout the state and later on a national Chautauqua circuit. With the help of a school superintendent, he went from first grade to a college degree in four years. "He took a great interest in me. I worked hard to make progress, and his extra help and encouragement made that progress possible."

Andrew Paulson came in 1871 — broke, having lost everything in bad business deals in Wisconsin. His wife refused to wait until living conditions improved. She hopped a construction train for Ft. Abercrombie. As the story is told by daughter Jennie, "While mother lived near the river, she continued to make soap for the fort. She liked to do it, and it meant more money for her to keep house." Paulson valued education. He "succeeded in getting the settlers to send their children to the public school during the time it was open and sending them to religious and Norwegian school when the other school was closed." Jennie married a teacher who worked the land as well.

When he arrived in northwestern Dakota in 1887, Ole Sims found the ground covered with buffalo bones at White Earth, "so named because the ground was white with bones." Ole said Williston was just a shack and saloon from which drunks would stagger. Ole came to work on the railroad and stayed to homestead and farm. He recalls many disasters, any one of which might have driven less resilient homesteaders from the country. When a tornado tore off the roof of the granary where his boys were sleeping, they started to climb the walls. Ole told them to stay. But they had to run for safety "when a stack of hay started to blow into the building." Ole was lucky, for crop failure did not come to his area until 1931, "the first time in the history of our community that the land produced nothing at all."

Hans Siverts and his family, on the banks of the Knife River, endured hot, hot summers and blizzards so severe in the winter that they even allowed a dog to join them in the shack their first Christmas on the homestead. Mrs. Siverts remembers entertaining Indians who traveled to Dickinson and passed her homestead. When she saw one Indian who was in her home waiting out a rain storm bow before a statue of Christ she had in the room, she says, "If I had known . . . I would never have been afraid of them." She concludes, "In the years gone by I have learned, and my personal belief is, that the Indians are of good stuff. There never would have been any war between the red and the white man if the white man had been fair in all his dealings with the red man."

The Norwegian homesteaders certainly had the right stuff to make it in Dakota, and those who emigrated from Norway played a major role in establishing the schools and churches and government institutions enjoyed by their children's children.

The Norwegians in North Dakota History

D. Jerome Tweton

The Norwegian homesteader's story is entwined with the development of North Dakota.

We can learn much about our state by reading about the Norwegian experience on the land.

THE GREAT DAKOTA BOOM was on! Between 1878 and 1890 the population of North Dakota skyrocketed 1,000 percent — from 16,000 to 191,000. Of those who moved into the northern part of Dakota Territory during the boom, over 81,000 were European and Canadian immigrants. And of those, 26,000 were Norwegians. After the economically depressed 1890s, the Second Boom was on. By 1910 when North Dakota's population reached 577,000, over 123,000 claimed Norwegian as their mother tongue (21 percent of the state's population). North Dakota had clearly become a haven for land-seeking Norwegians. By 1915, as the map shows, Norwegians were located in every county and their farmland totaled 7,866,140 acres, about one-fifth of the farmland in the state.

Why North Dakota? The answer is simple. If one wanted free land with the potential of reasonable agricultural production, there was no other place to go. North Dakota was the farmer's last frontier. The

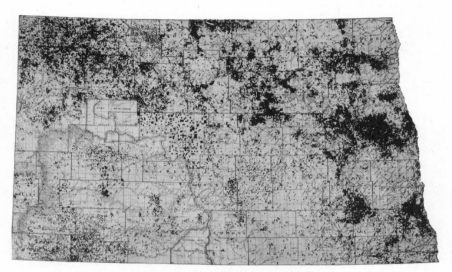

Land Owned by Norwegians in 1914
Courtesy of the University of North Dakota Special Collections, Chester Fritz Library.

good farmland in Iowa; eastern Kansas, Nebraska, and South Dakota; and Minnesota had been taken. Besides, northern Dakota's reputation as a fertile region had been widely touted. The Northern Pacific Railroad called it, "the northern banana belt." Territorial officials boosted it as a "Garden of Eden." The success of the vast bonanza farms proved that this was a wonderful place to grow wheat. How could a Norwegian go wrong in God's country?

The sixteen Norwegian sod-busters who are included in this book are representative of the Norwegian immigrant experience. They richly chronicle what life was like on the North Dakota frontier; they tell us about "the way it was." From their observations about pioneer life, we are able to draw several conclusions that enhance our understanding of the immigrant experience in general and the Norwegian in particular:

1) Very few Norwegians went directly to Dakota upon arrival in the United States. Some successfully farmed in Minnesota or Iowa or Wisconsin, sold out, and reinvested in North Dakota where land was free. Others worked to save up enough to start farming in North Dakota. The land may have been free, but one had to have somewhere in the neighborhood of $600 or $800 to

Christ Nelson sod house, Soper Post Office, North Dakota, 1896
Sod house with a wooden lean-to, stovepipe and one window showing. Five bicycles are
against the side of the addition. Eight people in the foreground from left to right:
George Bakken, Edwin Gjevre, John A. Lind, Thomas Haugen, Christ O. Nelson
(owner), John Erickson, Herman Haugen (on the roof), Martin Erickson. There are
also saw horses, a shoe on the roof, and tin cans and trash on the ground. 1896.

purchase the necessary lumber, food, oxen, horses, and basic implements to start a farming operation. For example, Peter Anderson who farmed in Eddy and later in Wells County, came to
America in 1880 and worked in Wisconsin as a general and farm
laborer for almost six years. "By being very saving," he recalled, "I
had enough money to buy two teams, wagons, breaking plow, a
cow and lumber." Anders Elken, who also ended up in Wells
County, arrived in the country in 1885 and worked as a laborer
near Spring Grove, Minnesota for three years before heading to
Dakota. "I had steady work since my arrival in America and saved
my money," he observed. Hans Amble, prior to obtaining land
near Devils Lake in 1888, had saved money by working as a farmhand around Pelican Rapids, Minnesota for seven years. The Al-
stads whose land was not far from Pekin "returned home to Min-

nesota to work during harvest and threshing to make enough money to live through the winter."

2) Norwegians, like other immigrant groups, settled near their fellow country people when at all possible. The map clearly shows the Norwegian clusters. John Bagstad headed for the Norwegian Kaldor settlement on the Goose River. Thomas Alstad's settlement partners were Paul and Ole Vrem and Nils Haugen. Nels Arntzen went to Ransom County where "several families from Norway settled at that point." He even taught "Norwegian school." The Berg family's closest neighbors were Andrew Staven and Nels Gronback. Hans Amble's first stop on the way to Dakota was Otter Tail County, Minnesota where he stayed with "friends of the family from Norway." Although Louis (Larson) Froguer settled near a Devils Lake Jewish neighborhood, his closest farm associates were Hans and Martin Paulson, Adolph Olson, and Olavius Lundaas. Out in the northwest during the second boom Ole Sims worked closely with Rud Anderson, Oscar Storheim, Hans Hougland, Halvor Rue and Sven Sussage. This, of course, was a natural thing to do. In a strange land, the familiarity of language, customs, and faith gave the Norwegian and other ethnic groups great comfort. National camaraderie was a significant component of the immigrant experience.

3) During the years of the Dakota boom, the 1870s to 1890, river valleys especially attracted Norwegians. William Sherman in his 1983 North Dakota ethnic atlas called the Sheyenne River a "Norwegian river from southern Cass County, extending west and north for almost 200 miles until it reaches Wells County." The Goose River and its tributaries became an exclusively Norwegian settlement for the eighty-mile run of the valley. The Park and Forest rivers to the north also became Norwegian enclaves. Why? Food, water, fuel and building timber are the obvious answers. Thomas Alstad: "We were very fortunate to be so near the river where we got a large part of our food supply." Nicolai Berg: "The river offered the only good water." Nels Arntzen: "We cut wood for fuel at the Sheyenne River. . . ." Albert Hoiland: "During the summer of 1879, father built a house and barn, both of

logs. He felled trees in the timber along the Sheyenne and shaped the logs with an axe. . . ." The less obvious answer? Perhaps in this very flat country the valleys reminded the Norwegians of a little bit of Norway. As John Bagstad put it, "The Goose River was . . . a pretty sight to behold."

4) An amazing number of Norwegians used the land laws to gain more than the traditional 160-acre homestead. Three methods of obtaining government land were available. Under *pre-emption* (1841) a settler could purchase 160 acres for $1.25 per acre after living on the land for a year. Residence, cultivation and improvements had to be proved. Under the *Homestead Act* (1862) one could acquire 160 acres of free land provided he or she lived on the land, cultivated ten acres, and planted a crop. After five but less than seven years, the farmer had to present proof of compliance with the law — proving up. The land then became his or hers upon payment of nominal fees. The *tree claim* (Timber Culture Act, 1873) allowed a person to claim up to 160 acres in exchange for planting and maintaining 10 acres of trees and paying nominal fees, the person would gain title after eight years if he or she could prove that the tree planting had been successful. Several of the Norwegians in this volume worked the laws to gain 320 acres. Thomas Alstad proved his pre-emption in 1883 and then homesteaded an adjoining 160 acres. Hans Amble gained 320 acres through pre-emption and a tree claim. Peter Anderson employed all three laws. He pre-empted and tree claimed in Eddy County and homesteaded when he moved to Wells County. Ole Brenna filed on both a homestead and a tree claim near Grand Forks. Out west on the banks of the Knife River, Hans Siverts put together 320 acres through a homestead and a tree claim. Of course, land could be purchased from a railroad or land company. Aadne Hoiland, who had been a successful farmer and carpenter in Minnesota, purchased an entire section (640 acres) for $2.50 an acre. He also homesteaded an adjoining 160 acres.

Theodore Jerdine sod house, Osnabrock, North Dakota

Sod house with sod roof, stovepipe and three windows showing. Men from left to right: Christ Evenrude (hired hand), Lars Gvesrude, Theodore Jerdine. In the buggy: Mrs. Theodore Jerdine and her mother, Mrs. Gvesrude. Children sitting on the ground: Johanna, Thilda, Julia, and Rudolph. June 1906.

Sod house on Andrea Springan's claim by Williston, North Dakota

Four men and a woman in front of a sod house with a door and a stovepipe showing. From left to right: Andrea Springan, Henry Springan of Stanley, N.D., Tom Springan, Abraham Bjornstad of Hoople, N.D., and Jacob Rollefstad of Hoople, N.D. 190-?.

Helgeson Farm and sod house, southwest of Fairdale, North Dakota
Lewis Hanson's threshing crew
Main focus is on the threshing crew in the Helgeson farm yard. To left in background is
the sod house, and other wooden structures partially visible behind crew. On right is a
cook car with women and children in doorway. Men are on horses or in the hay rack.
Wagons are hitched to oxen and horses. There is a dog by the horses, and three women
are seated in a two-horse surrey. 190-?.

THE NORWEGIAN IMMIGRANT EXPERIENCE parallels the
entire North Dakota settlement era which stretched nearly fifty years
from the early 1870s up to World War I. They were among the first settlers during the Great Dakota Boom and among the last settlers during
the Second Boom. From Andrew and Hanna Paulson who took land in
1872 near Ft. Abercrombie on the Wild Rice River down to Louise
Woodwick and Dusty La Mont who homesteaded near Haynes in 1905,
the Norwegian homesteader story in entwined with the development of
North Dakota. We can learn much about our state by reading about the
Norwegian experience on the land.

Going Broke, Bouncing Back

Thomas J. Alstad

It will take such a __ __ long time to get back to where I was last night before the storm.

Thomas J. Alstad was born in Hevne, Norway on October 26, 1855. In May 1868, his father, Johan, took Thomas and his brother, John, to America. The three Alstad men found farm work around Mankato, Minnesota, and within a year had saved enough money to bring Mrs. Alstad and two daughters to Minnesota. Johan Alstad homesteaded in Chippewa County not far from Granite Falls. Thomas met Anne Hagen, the daughter of a nearby farmer. Anne had migrated from Stangwik, Norway with her parents in 1868. They fell in love and married in December 1874. Thomas had purchased 80 acres near his father. Several poor seasons sent Alstad in search of greener pastures: Dakota. The Alstad story demonstrates that land seekers often claimed their homesteads quite a distance from the nearest railroad.

AS SOON AS I GOT MARRIED, I started farming for myself. In the spring of 1875 I put in my first crop and started to build a house on the land. My wife stayed with her parents while I was building the house. Our first child, a girl, was born there near Mankato, Minnesota.

The grasshoppers came and destroyed the crop before I completed the house, but I built it anyway and kept on farming. I put in crops every

1

spring, and the grasshoppers cleaned me out every year for three successive seasons. They did not bother the crops in 1879 and 1880, but the harvest was poor, anyway, so I sold the farm and got enough out of it to pay debts. We lived with our two children (our son James was born June 12, 1879) that winter and the spring of 1881 with my wife's parents. Then I started out for Dakota Territory along with Ole and Paul Vrem, Lars Loe, Bernt Opoien, Halvor Johnson, and my brother-in-law, Nils Eagen. We had four teams of horses and four prairie schooners — owned by me, Ole and Paul Vrem, and Nils Hagen. We went through Benson, Fergus Falls, and Moorhead, Minnesota. We crossed the Red River on a ferry between Moorhead and Fargo and went on to Valley City, which was just a small village.

We bought some rough lumber at Valley City, about enough for the floors and doors of the cabins we planned to build on our claims, as well as enough for benches, cupboards and bunks. From Valley City we struck out in a northwesterly direction along the Sheyenne River, crossed the prairie where Cooperstown was eventually established, and went to the Bue Post Office. There were no white settlers west of this place, except for a few who came at the same time we did. But there were half-breeds who claimed squatter's rights to some of the land close to where we lived. Bernt Opoien and Nils Hagen liked that particular location, so they bought out the half-breeds, and each of us squatted on 160 acres of land along the river bank. We got logs from the trees along the river banks and built a cabin on each claim, all about the same size — about 14 by 16 feet, with sod roofs and one small window and one door in each cabin. We had some of our machinery and household goods shipped from Minnesota to Valley City — harrows, rakes, mowers, stoves, and tables. We hauled them from Valley City to our cabins.

My claim was the E½ of the NW¼ and W½ of the NE¼ of section 32, township 150, Range 60. The other claims adjoined mine. As soon as we completed the cabins, we cut some hay and broke a few acres on each farm with breaking plows we purchased on our way in Fargo.

We returned to Minnesota to work during harvest and threshing to make enough money to live through the winter. While there, we stayed with our wives' families. On the first of November three of us started our second trip to Dakota Territory. We stopped at Valley City again and purchased what we thought would be enough provisions to last all winter. We arrived at the cabins on November 20th. As the weather was mild, we started right to work and built stables for our stock and fixed up our houses for the winter.

Along toward the latter part of December, our provisions started to run low, so I and a neighbor, Ole Raagen, took a team and drove to the nearest town, Valley City, to get a new supply. There were no roads of any kind, and the weather was rather stormy, so traveling was very difficult. We got there, bought what groceries we could with the little money we had, and returned to our claims. But the trip to town for groceries took about two weeks.

We were very fortunate to be so near the river where we got a large part of our food supply. There were plenty of fish in the river and a large number of cottontail rabbits and prairie chickens in the woods. We had no trouble catching plenty of fish to eat, and prairie chickens we could get right from the steps of the cabin. I used a double-barreled muzzle-loading shotgun for shooting the chickens at night, and I could shoot the ones sitting on the lower limbs of the trees without even scaring the others away. We couldn't afford to use our ammunition for shooting the cottontails, so we snared them. We would have gone hungry quite a bit of the time during the first winter if it had not been for the wild game there.

Early in the spring of 1882, I drove to Minnesota with my team and covered wagon and brought my family out to our claim in Dakota Territory. Osago Township was surveyed in the fall of 1881 and spring of 1882. The squatters went to Grand Forks to file claims. I went in the spring to sign up, and while I was there, I sold my horses and bought three oxen, because they could keep in good condition with only prairie grass to eat whereas horses have to have grain, which was very hard to get at that time.

That spring I put in my first crop in Dakota Territory, five acres of wheat. The grain matured in good condition, the kernels were large and plump. I had no reaper of my own, but a neighbor, Lars Loe, had one, so I hired him to cut the grain. There was no threshing rig available that fall, so the grain remained unthreshed during the winter of 1882-1883. I had about 25 acres ready to be seeded in the spring, but I had no money and no seed, except for the grain still in the bundles. I realized that the only way I could get the necessary seed would be to flail it out of the wheat I had raised the year before. To get the wheat separated from the straw and chaff, I had to have a hard, smooth floor to work on. My brother-in-law had a shack down by the river that was unoccupied at that time, so I carried water from the river and poured it on the floor and let it freeze — hard and smooth. I made flails and beat out about 25 or 30 bushels of wheat. It was very hard, slow work, but I finally got enough seed for about 30 or 35 acres.

I used that seed in the spring of 1883 and put in about 20 or 25 acres of wheat on my own land and about ten additional acres on some land I rented from B.S. Opoien. The crop was good, about 35 bushels to the acre. I do not remember the exact price, but it was from 80 to 90 cents a bushel. I hauled the grain to Michigan City, which was 25 miles northeast of my farm, and purchased groceries and supplies there.

I proved up my pre-emption claim that fall and took a homestead claim on the adjoining quarter. I broke up some land on the homestead the next year and put in about 30 acres of wheat. The crop looked good. I was ready to harvest it on the next Monday, but a Saturday night storm hailed me out. I felt pretty blue and went over to one of my neighbors, Joseph Pierce. He had 200 acres of wheat, had just purchased two new binders, and had made one round on his wheat field before he was hailed out. I learned later that the hail storm had covered a large territory and that most of the farmers in my territory had been cleaned out. When I talked to Joseph Pierce about the hailstorm, he said, "I suppose we'll live through it all right, but it will take such a _____ _____ long time to get back where I was last night before the storm."

Money was scarce that fall, but I continued farming and had some fair crops the next few years. I broke up a few additional acres each year and seeded all the land to wheat. After fair crops in 1884 and 1885, I put in about 150 acres of wheat in 1886 and got more than 30 bushels to the acre. The wheat was very clean, no weed seeds of any kind at the time. It was the best crop I ever had in North Dakota. I put in 150 acres again in 1887, but had just a small crop because of the drought.

In 1888, I borrowed $1,000 from a land company and gave them a mortgage of $500 on each of my quarter-sections. I bought 40 acres adjoining my first claim, some horses and machinery, and then put in about 150 acres of wheat. The crop came along fine, and all the farmers thought they would get good returns for the work they had put in on their farms, but about the middle of August all the grain froze. We farmers got nothing for our year's labor. I was forced to let the land company take my land because I had no money to pay off the mortgage.

I rented the Ottofy farm, 320 acres, in the fall of 1888. I also ran a small general store in the building formerly used as the Ottofy Post Office. The children were old enough by this time to help us folks with the work, so we didn't need much outside help. We had some good crops, but we also made money in the store business. Everything was running smoothly, and our family was very contented when one of the greatest tragedies of our lives struck. I and my son, James, about seventeen years old, were in the store one evening when a thunder storm came up. Lightning struck the building and killed my boy, standing just a few feet away from me. It took me years to get over that.

We continued farming at that place for several years. About 1898 we bought two quarters of land — the southwest quarter of section 22 and the northwest quarter of section 27 in the same township, Osago, and farmed there for several more years.

In 1906 the railroad came through that territory and crossed the southwest quarter of our land. The railroad decided to locate the town Pekin there, and I sold the town 40 acres of land at $50 per acre with an agreement that I would buy back any land they didn't use. The town did not spread out very much, and I later bought back a number of acres.

In 1908 we quit farming, built a house in Pekin, and moved there.

When a Norwegian Marries a Swede

Hans and Betsy Amble

We lived in this sod house for fifteen years and reared our family of eight children there.

In 1882 the Lars Amble family emigrated to America, joining other Norwegians in Otter Tail County, Minnesota, near Pelican Rapids. One of four children, Hans Amble was born on October 15, 1861. Betsy Amble was born in Carlstad, Sweden, on January 6, 1866. Her parents, Herman and Sophia Ross, had ten children, all of whom left Sweden for the United States. Betsy was a delicate child; and, had it not been for the untimely death of her mother, she might never have come to America as did her brothers and sisters. When Betsy was 15 in 1881, she joyously accepted a free passage ticket to Minneapolis where her generous sister, Amanda, lived. Eight years later Amanda and Betsy went to Dakota where they stayed at the farm home of William Gamble. Here Betsy, while convalescing from typhoid fever, met Hans Amble. They married after a brief courtship.

ARRIVED IN THIS COUNTRY from Norway in 1882. I was a young lad just past my twentieth birthday and knew very little of the world to which I had come. My trip on the ocean was uneventful. I came over just like the rest of the emigrants did. I landed in New York and took the train for Otter Tail County, Minnesota, where friends of the family from Norway were located. Their names

A Type of early American architecture on the North Dakota prairie
Man standing by entry of sod house. Two windows and stovepipe visible. Woodpile, saw, and wooden buckets beside house. Supporting beams extend out of house. To right is a person standing beside two hitched oxen. Axvig sod house, Milton, North Dakota, 188-?.

were Ole Onsum and Theodore Eagstad. I made my home at Ole Onsum's whenever I was out of work. I came to America because some friends had come before me, and I heard of the free land in America. I stayed around Pelican Rapids, Minnesota, from 1882 until 1885, working as a farmhand. In 1885 I went to the William Gamble farm, three miles north of Fargo. I worked at the Gamble farm until harvest and threshing season from 1885 until 1889. I spent the rest of my time at Ole Onsum's farm near Pelican Rapids, Minnesota. I did chores and any other work there was to do for board and room.

In 1888 I made a trip to Devils Lake to look over the country, with the view of locating a piece of land on which to stake a claim. I walked from Devils Lake to Rolette County. I found the claim on which my sister and husband, Mr. and Mrs. Bernt Haagenson, were living. After looking over the country, I went back to Devils Lake and filed on my pre-emption in SW¼ section 17 and tree claim NE¼ section 19, Rice Township, on June 2, 1888. I hired Bernt Haagenson to break ten acres for me on the pre-emption, and on the tree claim I had trees planted. I returned again to Fargo to work on the Gamble farm.

In the fall of 1889 I met Miss Betsy Ross. We were married on January 5, 1890. After a short honeymoon spent with friends in Pelican Rapids and Kragnes, Minnesota, and Fargo, we came west to Rugby enroute to our homestead. We were met at Rugby by a neighbor, J.T. Twe-

7

**One of the last sod barns in use in Walsh County,
built in late 1880s**

*Six head of cattle (oxen?) in a pasture in front of a sod-roofed building. There
appears to be an open entry area, and part of wall is supported by wood. Along
side is a wire fence and a gate. Last sod house in Walsh County
(Weberg-Dubois). Late 1800s, 191-?.*

ten, who took us to the home of my sister, Mrs. Bernt Haagenson. We arrived on March 1, 1890. With the help of Mr. Haagenson and Carl Hanson, I erected a sod shack, and we moved into our first new home on the prairies on March 10, 1890. The first room was 16 by 20 feet, but we added another room 10 by 12 feet. We plastered the walls with prairie clay. The floors were of lumber. It was a typical sod house, such as were the homes of our neighbors on the surrounding claims. We lived in this sod house for fifteen years and reared our family of eight children there.

The crops on the homestead, from 1888 to 1892, were anything but encouraging. The first crop in 1890 was a total failure from drought, frost, and gophers. I broke fifteen acres more that year, and it dried out. The first year we harvested a good crop was in 1905. With the crop production steadily mounting, conditions improved, and we built better homes and helped build a church and schoolhouse.

Pre-empting, Tree Claiming and Homesteading in Eddy and Wells Counties

Peter B. Anderson

We read newspapers and books which were passed from home to home.

> Peter B. Anderson was born in the parish of Vefsen, Northland, Norway on December 12, 1859. All of his ancestors, going back generations, had been farmers in the Northland area. Like so many young lads, he took the cattle to the mountains for the spring, summer, and fall and attended school for two to three months during the winter. He went to high school for two years while he worked for neighboring farmers. Like most Norwegian immigrants he arrived in the United States with not much more than the shirt on his back. And, like most of the others, he worked hard somewhere to the east of Dakota to earn a stake, illustrating that the land might have been free or cheap but one needed at least $500 to start farming.

HEN I WAS TWENTY YEARS OF AGE, the urge came to me to make my own living. I felt sure that my folks, realizing that the opportunities in Norway were quite limited, would manage to get along without my help. Hence, in 1880, I came to America. I arrived in Wisconsin the same year, where I remained until 1886, working in different parts of the state at general and farm labor. Most of my winters were spent working in the woods. In the fall of 1885 I journeyed to Dakota Territory and filed on a pre-emption and tree claim, the E½ of section 32, township 148, range 62 (Eddy County). I then returned to Wisconsin to work in the woods during the winter.

On April 5, 1886, I married Miss Anna Jahnson. I and my young bride came to the claim in Dakota Territory, arriving in Cooperstown on April 9th.

By being very saving, I had enough money to buy two teams, wagons, breaking plow, a cow and lumber for a shack and stable, which was crudely built and mostly of sod. The lumber and other materials for building and furnishing the little house were hauled thirty miles with a team and wagon. I built the house myself a frame building 12 by 20 feet, consisting of two rooms, with one window in each room, a door in the partition between the two rooms, and one outside door.

I made all of the furniture. We bought a cook stove and the cooking utensils — very few — in Cooperstown. We had one small kerosene lamp for light and two gallons of kerosene that had to last all winter; no light was used during the other seasons as we arose at daylight and retired at twilight. The fuel we used consisted mostly of brush obtained along the hillsides and in the gullies; the balance of it consisted of cow chips and hay.

We used oxen 100 percent for the field work. But for road work, they were rather slow, and they found it more difficult to go through snow than horses. Therefore, we had to get all of our farm produce to market and get our fuel and other supplies home before the snow came. Skis were used a great deal during the winter when we did not have to transport more than one hundred pounds, which we tied in a compact bundle and put on our backs for the journey.

Aside from cold weather, blizzards and deep snow during the winters, we had to fight prairie fires every fall. Land seekers and hunters were careless because they did not thoroughly extinguish their campfires, and a hard wind would often fan an ember into flame and light the dry grass which extended many miles in every direction. In order to protect our homes and grain fields, we plowed wide fire breaks around them. Even then, the fire often would throw sparks across the fire breaks and make it necessary for us to make backfires in order to protect our homes. We often said that a prairie fire, on a windy day, could travel faster than a horse could run.

When a fire started, there was no chance for rest until it was put out. Water barrels, plenty of sacks and even old coats had to be handy for immediate use on such an occasion. The barrel, filled with water, was placed on a stone boat or in a wagon and drawn up to the fire line. The sacks and old articles of clothing were dipped into the water and used to beat the fire out. Men, women and children took part in fire fighting.

The nearest trading points were were Carrington, New Rockford, and Cooperstown, each about thirty miles distant. We bought all of our groceries and other supplies at Cooperstown — before the heavy snows of winter came. All perishable foods were stored in cellars to prevent spoiling. We had a separate cellar for our cream and milk.

Climatic conditions made life very dangerous. Even on clear days, the fiercest storms sometimes started within a few hours. During our first winter on our homestead, the snow was very deep. The roads were blocked to such an extent that it was impossible to make the trip to town. Much of traveling at such a time was done on skis. Two men made the trip to town and transacted all the neighborhood's business. Some of the storms lasted as long as 72 hours, after which the barn and other buildings would often be completely covered with snow. It would take hours of hard labor to dig our way through the snow to take care of the stock. Sometimes the stock went three days at a time without feed.

I had four oxen and a sixteen-inch breaking plow to break up the land. No feed was necessary for the oxen, as they were worked for only three or four hours at a time and were then allowed to graze for a few hours before they were put back to work. I seeded my first crop by hand and had it cut with a binder by one of my neighbors. It was not a very abundant crop — but none of my others were either, because of the adverse climatic conditions.

Some of my neighbors in Eddy County were Knute Alfstad, Torsten Alfsted, Nels Hove, Knute O. Melby, Ole K. Melby, Torlef Roble, and

Ole S. Hove. When I wished to visit one of my neighbors four or five miles away, I would hitch the oxen to the wagon early in the morning and get an early start because the oxen were very slow walkers, and there would be little time left for visiting. A ten-mile trip usually took all of one day.

From 1887 to 1895 farm products were quite low in price: wheat sold as low as 30 cents per bushel, barley as low as 9 cents; eggs were from 5 to 8 cents per dozen, and butter sold for from 5 to 8 cents per pound. However, a five dollar bill went a long way in buying other articles — coffee cost from 12 to 15 pounds for a dollar, flour from $2.50 to $2.75 per hundredweight, salt from a half to one cent per pound, and tobacco from 50 to 75 cents per pound.

The only active recreation we enjoyed while we were living on our claim in Eddy County was an occasional dance at one of the neighborhood homes. We danced in a small, 12- by 12- or 14- by 14-foot room. Penny ante was played to some extent by the men. For pastime, we read newspapers and books which were passed from home to home in the community. Later on, debates were held.

In 1892, I made a trip to what is now the township of Manfred, Wells County, where I found and filed on a 160-acre homestead. The following year we left Eddy County, after proving up on the pre-emption and taking a loan of $300 on the land. It cost me $240 to make the final proof, leaving me $60. That was all I received for my farm, so I let the loan company foreclose.

In 1893, we moved to the new homestead where I built a new home. While on this homestead, I purchased other adjoining land that proved very fertile and a profitable investment. Here we stayed, and we did very well.

Trouble with an Irishman

Nels Arntzen

He caught her and killed her with the spade.

Nels Arntzen, accompanied by his wife and three children, left Trondheim in June 1882 on the Maltha*. After fifteen days they landed in Boston. The trip was too much for two-month-old Arnie Arntzen. He died shortly after landing in America. The Arntzens took the train to Casselton and went to Owego, Ransom County, where many Norwegians had already settled since the mid-1870s. The Arntzen family illustrates a significant point about getting land, the right land. They moved three times: first to a squatter's claim, then to a homestead, then to land that they purchased outright. Presumably, each time they located on more suitable farm land. This was not an uncommon practice of the settlement process.*

WE LEFT NORWAY IN JUNE 1882 and sailed from Trondheim, Norway, on the *Maltha*, and landed in Boston after about fifteen days of sailing. I was accompanied by my wife and three children. The youngest child, Arnie, was but two months old. The voyage was too much for him, and he died shortly after we landed in Boston.

We went by rail to Casselton, Dakota, and from there to Owego in Ransom County. There were several families from Norway settled at that point, and for the first winter, 1882-83, I taught Norwegian school at this place.

Trouble with an Irishman

Among the goods that we brought with us from Norway was one bed, one chair, all of our bedding, clothing, and dishes. These we shipped from St. Paul to Casselton. From there, we hauled our belongings to our claim in Milnor Township, section 30. Here we built a 14- by 16-foot sod and lumber shack. I made a table, benches, and bought a small stove in Milnor. We cut wood for fuel at the Sheyenne River or bought it in Milnor.

We later moved to Weber Township in 1886 where we took a homestead in the NW¼ of section 6. Here we lived for five years. Then we bought a 275-acre farm in Rutland Township where we lived permanently.

The first winter that we spent in our sod house in Milnor Township was very cold, and there was a great deal of snow. We were quite comfortable in the house, but getting to town for provisions and fuel was sometimes a problem. On one occasion when my brother-in-law and I went to the river after wood, we were caught in a blizzard. We were on our way back with our load, but we could not see where we were going. We happened to run onto a straw stack, which provided some shelter for our oxen. We dug ourselves into the straw, where we had to stay all night. Our greatest difficulty was keeping awake, for I am sure if we had gone to sleep, we would have frozen to death. I had to fight with my brother-in-law all night to keep him awake. The next morning the storm had let up enough so that we could get home. We froze our fingers and feet quite badly. In this same storm, one of my neighbors froze his feet and lost one of his oxen when he was caught on his way home from Milnor.

On another occasion, while living in Weber Township, a number of us went together to the Indian Reservation [Sisseton] to get wood. It was a nice warm day, and we were not dressed very warmly. We had loaded our wagons and had started for home when a storm struck us. The temperature went down to below zero. The wind blew so hard that it was almost impossible to walk against it. We were out in this storm all night. We didn't know where we were going, but had to keep on, as there was no place to stop. The oxen followed the trail without our help, and we arrived safely home the next morning. Our clothes were frozen stiff, and I nearly lost my eyesight. I had to stay in bed several days. Al-

Descendants of the original inhabitants of Dakota Territory
*Two Native Americans standing in front of tipis, with tents and other Native Americans
in background. Likely taken by Job V. Harrison of Rock Lake, N.D. , 190-?.*

though we all nearly froze to death, none of us suffered any permanent
effect, as we were all young and strong and full of vigor.

The Indians on the reservation were a constant worry to some settlers who lived close by. Every once in a while they would have a pow-
wow, or war dance. On these occasions the settlers would be ready to
flee at any sign of trouble, but nothing ever happened.

The Ft. Sisseton to Ft. Ransom government trail crossed the Wild
Rice River between sections 5 and 6. It was not used by the government
as late as 1886, when we lived in Weber Township, but the trail was used
by the settlers. It followed a southeasterly direction across Weber
Township.

On the southeast shore of Sprague Lake, in Rutland Township, a
town named Sprague Lake was started in 1886. There were two stores,
two saloons, a blacksmith shop and other buildings. The Great Northern Railway Company had graded from Cayuga, but the road was later
changed to go through Rutland. Most of the town was moved there.

The Wild Rice River, which crosses Weber Township, overflowed its banks in the spring of 1888, filling up all sloughs and low places for miles around. Some of these sloughs never dried up again.

An Irishman by the name of Cody had filed on a claim a few miles south of us. He was living there with his daughter. A bachelor by the name of Crosby lived several miles east. Crosby was quite interested in Miss Cody, but his attentions were very unwelcome to both Mr. Cody and his daughter.

One evening Crosby came to pay a visit, but as always, was not very welcome. A neighbor named Mike Doyle was also calling on the Codys that evening, so Doyle induced Crosby to leave with him. They had not gone very far when Crosby suddenly turned around and ran back to the house. He grabbed a spade, smashed in a window, and jumped through it. Miss Cody ran out of the door, but he caught her and killed her with the spade. He then went after Mr. Cody, but by this time Doyle had returned to the house. Between the two men, they got the spade away from Crosby, who started across the prairie. He stayed overnight at Charles Larson's, and the next day was arrested and taken to Wahpeton. Several days later he committed suicide by hanging himself in his cell.

John E. Bagstad

Kaldor Settlement on the Goose River

John E. Bagstad

The Goose River section was heavily timbered and a pretty sight to behold.

The Erik J. Bagstad family left Norway in May 1881. John E. Bagstad was four months short of his eleventh birthday. The Bagstads, like most Norwegian families, intended to find land in an area where Norwegians had already established a farming community. Their destination was the Kaldor settlement not far from Hillsboro on the Goose River in what would become Norway Township. The Kaldor families had opened up the Goose River country in the early 1870s.

ON THE MORNING OF THE SECOND DAY OUT, just a few of the highest mountain peaks of Norway were visible. The passengers were on deck watching the last sign of the fatherland disappear in the distance. The trip across the North Sea to England took about three days. There were no cabins on the boat, but there were several large rooms with bunks constructed out of rough lumber and built one above the other. There were no tables or chairs. We passengers had to sit on our bunks or trunks. Meals were served from large boilers carried into the room by the waiters. We had to furnish our own cups, plates, knives and forks and sit on our bunks or trunks while eating. The air was very bad most of the time.

The boat docked at Hull, and the trip across England to Liverpool was made by rail. At Liverpool we boarded a White Star Line steamer, the *Majestic*. This boat was also a steamer, but it carried lots of sail. Conditions on this boat were about the same as on the North Sea boat. The trip across the Atlantic took 13 or 14 days. We had to provide our own straw beds and blankets, and the last night on board we slept without the straw beds because we were ordered to throw them overboard before the boat docked.

In New York, we were taken to a place called Castle Garden and kept there for about two days for medical examination. At New York, passengers for the West boarded a special train for Chicago. The coaches were old and dirty, and the seats were wooden slats. Coaches were locked all the time so nobody would get lost. At Chicago we passengers for the Northwest were put on a special train for St. Paul. We spent lots of time on sidings because other traffic had the right of way. At St. Paul our family was put on board a regular passenger train for Fargo, Dakota Territory — as far as our tickets took us. From Fargo, rails had been laid as far as the Goose River in Traill County, and we made the last part of the journey on a supply train that was backed out of Fargo north to the Goose River. A townsite, Hill City, now called Hillsboro, had been laid out on the Goose River the previous fall, and quite a few business places had started: Hans Johnson, general merchandise; John E. Paulson, machinery; Gunder Howard, machinery; and Plummer & Hanson, banking.

Our destination was the Kaldor settlement on the Goose River, about eight miles northeast of Hill City, and one of the early settlers, Lars Overmoen, took us there with a team of horses and a lumber wagon.

The Goose River section was heavily timbered and a pretty sight to behold, but we missed the hills and mountains of Norway. The settlers' houses along the river were built out of logs, and most of them were thatched with bark with a covering of sod on top. Out on the prairie there were a number of sod houses and a few tarpaper shanties. Very little of the prairie had been broken, probably because the market was too far away. The nearest was Fargo, and it took several days to make the trip there with a load of wheat, even for those who had horses. With oxen it took more than a week.

The first Monday after we arrived, I was enrolled as one of the pupils in the school, Schoolhouse No. 3. There was a three-month term

Rural school near Osnabrock, North Dakota
Interior of school with children lined up in front of school, teacher at left, 190-?.

that had already started. The school building had been constructed out of logs that spring, donated by M.O. Kaldor, C.O. Kaldor, A.O. Kaldor, Simon Kaldor, Lars Moen, Hans A. Moen and Lars Bakkum. All had timber on their claims. The school had been erected by donation work under the supervision of Simon and Anders Kaldor who were experienced log builders from Norway. Some of the homesteaders on the prairie also donated work. It was a building of about 16- by 24-feet which had a door at the end and two windows on each side. The fixtures were homemade benches with a shelf in front on which to keep books and do the writing. There was a reading chart, a map of the United States, and a homemade blackboard. The hind leg of a jack rabbit was provided for an eraser. The floor was wide rough boards thrown in loose — not nailed down. The ground where the building stood was uneven so the wind would blow under the building and up through the cracks in the floor. But it was summertime, so it did not matter.

Sometimes when the teacher did not arrive to unlock the door, the pupils crawled under the building and lifted up two of the center boards and got in that way. When the teacher arrived, he found all the pupils seated. The first teacher was O.E. Loe. He was a good teacher and a good singer. He also had a small house organ that he owned, and he played for the pupils while we sang. He taught geography this way: there was a large map of the United States, and the teacher would point to the different states. We pupils would recite the names in unison, as well as the capitals, large cities, boundaries of the states and main rivers. After a lesson, all the pupils would turn their backs to the map and recite the names of the states, how they were bounded, the capitals, the larger cities, etc. We learned a whole lot about the United States of America in this fashion. Before the school was erected, short terms had been taught at the farm house of Reverend Jonas Ostlund.

Before fall, a permanent floor was put in the school building, and a large box stove was installed for heating. A short term of parochial school was held during the winter of 1881-1882. The following spring a regular term of school was held.

This log school house was used for about five years and was then torn down and replaced by a frame building on the same site. A few years later this building was struck by lightning and burned down. Then a brick building with full basement was erected. This did not last long either, because the bank started to slide and the building cracked up and had to be torn down. Then another frame building, the fourth school, was erected on the same site.

Aal's Congregation, the first church, had been organized in 1872 by Reverend B.L. Hagebø, a minister who traveled in the territory. He swam the Red River, crossing from Minnesota into Dakota Territory, and journeyed up the Goose River to the settlement in Norway Township in 1872, the year before the first settlers arrived. The few settlers gathered at Lars E. Moen's log house on a Sunday where they held the first services and organized the congregation. For a few years, Reverend Hagebø held occasional services for the pioneers.

In the summer of 1881, plans for a church building were made; it was completed in 1882. The building contractor was Peter H. Wold. The cost of the structure was about $3,000. Prior to the erection of the church, services were held in homes.

During the summer of 1881, my father prepared to erect a log house on the SW¼-16-146-51, which he later bought. It was a building of about 12 by 14 feet which had two windows and one door. The furnishings consisted of four kitchen chairs, a Bismarck cook stove, ordinary cooking utensils, homemade table and beds, and other articles made by my father. Other improvements on the land consisted of a sod stable and a well. In the fall of 1882, father built a grain crib after he harvested ten acres of wheat and got 300 bushels. He had a yoke of oxen, a prairie breaker, and a drag. He broadcast seed for the first crop by hand. Harvesting was done by a self-raking reaper, owned by a neighbor, and the grain was bound with straw by hand. Threshing was done with a separator driven by horse power. Other farm animals were a cow and a calf, a pig, and seven chickens. Five years later we built an addition to the log house, about 16 by 24 feet. This formed a T-shaped building which we lived in until the summer of 1899, when a modern frame house was built.

The settlers had to depend upon their own resources for an existence. They were sturdy, hardworking people who bravely faced the hardships of pioneering. The women brought their spinning wheels with them. Several looms were built in the community, and women spun yarn and wove cloth, knit socks, mittens, caps, scarves and jackets, and made all the other clothing we wore. The men were just as independent. They made their own implements for tilling the soil, made wagons (*kubberuller*), sleighs, furniture and boats — all hewn out of Goose River timber. Christian O. Kaldor was an experienced tailor from Norway. He made the first pair of trousers that I got after arriving. Simon Kaldor was a trained shoemaker. The two made apparel for the men folk, who paid in trade work. Lars E. Moen was the trained blacksmith, and he took care of our needs in that line. He made his own blacksmith charcoal, and he was a genius in his line. He made several wooden clocks for settlers in the area. Settlers were social and helpful. If anyone was sick or in need, everybody would see to them and help out as best they could. It was very common for a settler to start on foot on a Sunday morning to call on the nearest neighbor, and neighbor after neighbor would join and make the rounds of the settlement to see how everybody was getting along. Our requirements were not so very great — a few sacks of flour for the winter, some green coffee, salt, sugar, syrup, dried apples and some spices — and we were all set for a six-month winter.

━━━━━━━━━━━

Opening Up Steele County

The Berg Family

Dairy products provided much of our food, and mother made butter, cheese and "prim."

> Halvor and Brita Berg came to America in 1853 and headed for Dane County, Wisconsin, an area heavily populated by Norwegians. Here three of their sons were born: the first died at age one. Nicolai, who tells the family's story, was born in 1856. His brother Joseph was born in 1859. That year, Halvor took his family to Northwood, Iowa, where he farmed for 17 years. In the fall of 1873 Halvor, who had heard "wonderful" claims about the Red River Valley, came to the unsettled territory of the upper Goose River Valley. Since the land had not been surveyed, he squatted on a claim and hired the closest neighbor to put up a hut, break some sod, and plant some potatoes. After the survey Halvor and Nicolai filed homesteads. Because the Bergs opened up Steele County for settlement, the post office and township were to be named New Berg; but, for unknown reasons, it became Newburgh.

━━━━━━━━━━━

O N MAY 24, 1874, FATHER, MOTHER, my brother Joseph (age 15) and I (age 18) left Iowa in a covered wagon for Dakota Territory, a distance of four hundred miles. We brought five milk cows, a bull, four calves, a yoke of oxen, a team of horses, a self rake reaper, a McCormick mower, a breaking plow, a broadcast seeder, and two narrow-tired wagons.

The journey took 28 days — we always rested on Sunday. The average day's drive was fifteen miles because the loads were heavy and the stock traveled very slow. Even at that, it was often necessary to take the young calves into the wagon.

Because of the heavy snow the previous winter and frequent rains in the spring, the Red River was very high. A ferry boat provided our only means of crossing when we arrived. When we reached the Sheyenne River, abut fifteen miles north of Fargo, there was no bridge, and the water was very high. The banks were flooded, but while we were deciding what was best to do, we found a private bridge about two miles out of our way. Three caravans met at this river crossing, and some of them refused to pay toll. But we Bergs paid, and we had a two days' lead on the others who did not. The other parties fixed up a wagon box so that it was waterproof. They used long poles cut from trees and tied them to the sides to help carry the load and balance the box. Women and children made up the last load, and the stock was forced to swim across.

Mother saw her share of hardship on this journey. Mosquitoes were very numerous and annoying due to the wet weather, and mother walked many miles per day as she helped drive the stock. She was very footsore at times. Saturday evenings, the men would seek a good place to camp over Sunday — always near a lake or stream so that there would be a good supply of water. The cook stove was taken out of the wagon so mother could bake bread enough to last a week. She always kept a supply of fermenting dough which she put with flour and warm water to make the bread. She had to wash clothes; and, often, the work of milking the cows fell to her. After we located, her tasks were not lessened.

We found the banks of the Goose River where we located steep and long. The river offered the only good water. It was over two years before we dug a well, so water for cooking and washing had to be carried a distance of 20 rods. We did not have a way to catch soft water from sod roofs, so women had to cleanse the hard water from the river with lye, which they made by soaking ashes in water and then straining it to make their own soft soap. Their hands got sore from the soap and scarcely had time to heal from one washing to the next. They made tubs by taking a block of hollow tree and covering the bottom with elm bark.

The prairie grass was full of fleas, and birds' nests often had bed bugs. Both of these pests made life miserable. Some of the first settlers did not even have a broom. They used a brush made of willows to brush away some of the extra dirt from the floor. When the men took a load of grain to Fargo, they took a week to make the trip. The wives and children left alone suffered great hardship. If a farmer raised a few hundred bushels of grain, it meant several trips because a full load was fifty bushels in sacks. Steamboats operated on the Red River between Moorhead and Winnipeg, the only marketing outlet for grain. Thirty to thirty-five bushes per acre was the average, and the price paid at Fargo was eighty cents per bushel for wheat. There was considerable rivalry among buyers, and they often would meet the farmers before they reached Fargo and offer them as much as a dollar and a half per bushel. After the coming of the railroads in the early 1880s, conditions improved in every way.

Dairy products provided much of our food. Mother made butter, cheese and "prim." Mush and milk was a common evening meal. When there was enough butter to sell, father took it to Caledonia, where he traded it for groceries and other necessities.

On July 4, 1874, my brother Joseph and I turned the first sod. We broke ten acres with oxen and spent the balance of the summer cutting trees to build a new log house. We hitched a yoke of oxen to the logs and hauled them with a long log chain to the place where we intended to build. Our building was sixteen by sixteen feet of rough logs with a dirt floor. Two years later we built a larger log house, 16 by 24, two stories high. That house became a favorite gathering place for the people of the community. My parents were most hospitable.

One day when the men worked at cutting logs in the sunshine, it became dark with a great swarm of grasshoppers. They devoured a patch of potatoes we had planted. They were so numerous down at the stream that they bent the willows down to the water, and many perished in this way. They stayed but a few days and then all rose, once again darkening the sun for a short time as they moved southward.

Early settlers on the upper Goose River found many unfavorable things which caused hardships, suffering and fear. There were prairie fires in summer and blizzards in winter. Settlers tried to protect themselves from prairie fires by breaking two furrows about a rod apart and burning grass between the furrows. But when the wind was blowing hard, it was not safe to do this because they feared the fire would get away from them. We pioneers watched for flashes of light across the horizon at night during the months of September and October. A big prairie fire swept through our area late in October 1874. It probably was started by sparks from an N.P. engine fifty miles south of the Goose River. At that time, there was not a settler between the river and the railroad. Fanned by a strong wind through at least two-years growth of tall grass, there was a great roar and dense smoke. The new settlers living on the south side of the river were very much frightened for good reason, because only small patches of land were broken, and they had no protection whatever.

Knute Paulson, a neighbor to the south of our place, saw the fire coming and climbed to the roof of his log cabin. He screamed, "Fire! Fire!" as loud as he could.

The main part of the fire went to the southeast, so what was left, we easily whipped out. Andrew Stavens and a young boy, Nels Gronback, age twelve, had a thrilling experience at this fire. They became entrapped and would have perished had it not been for the cool-headedness of Mr. Stavens, who wrapped wet sacks around himself and the boy. Even so, Mr. Stavens' hands and face were badly burned, and his eyes were so badly burned that he could not see for weeks.

Father inhaled so much heat and smoke while fighting prairie fires that he suffered weakened lungs. This had much to do with his early death at the age of fifty-three years.

Brother Joseph caused us much worry when he left with a team and wagon late in the fall of 1879 for Fargo to get a load of merchandise. A bad blizzard came up, and he had a narrow escape before finally reaching Fargo. We heard nothing from him for two weeks. He was forced to buy a bob sled in order to return home.

No one had screens on windows or doors, and only by keeping a smudge at the door were we able to stand it. When the stock came home at night in the summer, such a swarm would follow them that a smudge pot had to be brought into the house. With a brisk fire at the door, the flying pests could be coaxed out.

About 1880, father bought a Lambs Knitting Machine. Mother knit socks, stockings and mittens. After we sheared our sheep, we washed, carded and spun the wool on our spinning wheel. In 1882, a "New Home" sewing machine was purchased. Before this, mother made all clothing by hand. Tailor-made suits sold at the Newburgh Store for $15 to $25.

The first church services were held under the shade trees on father's homestead, less than two months after we Bergs arrived. We helped organize a congregation known as Hols Church. Ole Trageton and E. Nelson were chosen trustees, Knute Larson and Halvor Berg, deacons. Father was chosen to be secretary and treasurer. Services were conducted in the farm houses and in the open by students and ministers. Reverend Hageboe walked to and from his parishioners.

I was united in marriage to Miss Tonetta Heskin on November 21, 1874 in the first wedding in Steele County. We married in a 12- by 14-foot cabin of hewed logs which stood seven-feet high and was roofed with elm bark, and plastered with river-bottom clay. It had an earthen floor. It became our homestead home.

Our first child, Beatha, born August 27, 1875, was the first white girl born in Steele County. We had eleven children. Anna, age four, died in 1882; Halvor, age nine, died in 1902; and Nicolai, born in 1883, lived but a few hours.

Houses then were low and dark, and very few settlers had kerosene lamps. Some used a saucer full of lard with a cotton wick in it. Others made their own candles, but few had candle molds. They used the dipping process. Warm water was put into a deep vessel, and melted tallow was poured into the water. A piece of cotton cloth of suitable weight was dipped into this again and again until the settlers made a candle. They used candles to see to go to the barn after dark when necessary.

We cut hay with a scythe, and we had to cover our faces with cloth because of the mosquitoes.

There were only two grind stones in our township. Often women took scythes to be sharpened while men were having the noon meal and taking a little rest.

During the winter of 1879, an epidemic of diphtheria broke out in Newburg Township. There was no doctor within a hundred miles. A number of children died, including two of Paul Boe's; he buried them within a week. The Strands lost two and Glitres three. Kjemruds buried four during the winter.

The Hudson Bay Company built a large dam on the Goose River near Caledonia in 1874 for mill power, the only mill dam they built in Dakota Territory. This flour mill was of great value to the farmers of the upper Goose River.

The United States government began to survey the land in Steele County in 1875, and for those who had squatted on claims, it was of great importance to know where the lines would be between neighbor and neighbor. Disputes often arose which caused hatreds which lasted life times. The plats did not get back from Washington for a year, so no one could file a homestead before 1876. In June of that year, father and I started on foot to Fargo to file on the land we had been occupying. When we reached the Red River, we saw a steamboat bound for Fargo. Being weary and foot sore, we flagged the boat, which swung to the bank and picked us up. At nine o'clock the next morning, we appeared at the land office. The entrance fee was $15. The receiver questioned if I was old enough, but father explained that I was a married man. He allowed me to file. It took us four days to walk home.

Father established the first store in Steele County in 1876. Prior to this, settlers traded at Caledonia. The Morgan brothers, who ran a general store there, were of great help to settlers because they exchanged goods for products and also gave short-time credit when it was needed. They were of great help to father when he started his store. A post office was established at the store in 1877, and father was appointed postmaster. Mail came from Caledonia to all points between there and the store. The post office was discontinued in 1884, and people got their mail from Hatton.

Not until 1876 was there any grain to thresh. Before then, fields were small. With the kind of farm implements used, it was hard to pul-

**The Start of the busy season cutting grain on a farm
near Adams, North Dakota.**
*Four men and a boy binding and shocking grain. Two of the men have big bundles of
grain under their arms. There is a shock of grain beside them. Two teams of three horses
each are in the background and hitched to binders. One of the horse teams
has blankets on their backs, 190-?.*

verize the land. We had brought a self-rake reaper with us from Iowa,
and we were the only ones who had one. Our reaper would rake from
the platform of the binder enough straw for a bundle, and when the
reaper would come around, a man would bind this with straw. Some of
the settlers used a cradle, others a snath and scythe. These operated in
much the same way, but there was a sort of frame fastened to the snath
to catch the straw, which made it easier. If the field were large, four men
were stationed around it, and when the reaper would come around,
each would find a bundle and another would begin.

In 1878, McCormick harvesters came on the market. The grain was
elevated up, and the harvester was built in such a way that two men
could stand on the frame, each binding every other bundle and throw-
ing them off.

Many farmers had difficulty paying for their harvesters, which
could not be operated with oxen very well. So it was necessary to buy
horses at $400 or more per team, and some of the horses did not live
very long. Fargo was the nearest horse market. In the face of these ob-

stacles, farmers got into debt and had to borrow money and mortgage their property to meet their obligations. When a loan was granted, the terms were 12 percent and 6 percent bonus, payable in three years. When the money came, there was 18 percent and other expenses deducted from the principal, $12 per $100 paid in advance.

There was an Indian scare in the summer of 1879. Charles Mills, who lived near Casselton, sent word to the pioneers that the Canadian Indians were on the war path and threatening to exterminate the whites in the northeastern part of Dakota Territory. A special messenger, Halvor Thorson, came from Caledonia to warn Newburgh settlers of the danger. People became very nervous, and the young men prepared for the fight. They loaded their muskets, carbines and flintlock guns — all Civil War firearms — and were prepared to protect the settlers. We later learned that the Indians had left Canada to massacre the Red River settlers, but the mounted police drove them back. They were told that they belonged to Canada and would not be allowed to enter the United States.

James J. Hill, president of the Great Northern Railway Company, visited our area in September 1881. He had been on an inspection trip in the northern part of Dakota Territory. He traveled in a surrey drawn by horses. It happened that he arrived in Newburgh at noon, and he and his driver were invited to partake of the noonday meal, even though mother had a threshing crew to feed as well. Our twins were about six weeks old. They were in the box cradle covered with mosquito netting. Mr. Hill looked at them and then said, "Oh, they will vote for president" — a prophecy which came true.

Father died February 2, 1881, and mother on November 10, 1902. Two years before father's death, he selected a burial ground on his own land. He donated a piece of land on section sixteen, which has been incorporated as a cemetery. Sixteen people are buried there.

Early Arrivals in the Grand Forks Area

Kari Berg Brenna

We heard about the land in Dakota Territory and how we could get it . . .

When her uncle offered her a ticket to America in 1873, Kari Berg jumped at the opportunity to leave Norway. Born in 1856, she came from a family that farmed only a few acres and had a difficult time making a living. Karl's contribution to the family was making very good flat bread. She would go from farm to farm, stay for two or three days, and bake for the families. She had little schooling. Her father taught her how to read, and she learned how to write on her own. Ole Brenna, whom she would marry in 1877, arrived in the United States in 1869 and settled in the Rochester, Minnesota area where other members of his family were farming. The Brennas were among the first to locate south of Grand Forks, putting together a 320-acre farm through use of the Homestead Act and the Timber Culture Act.

I WORKED FOR MY UNCLE, Nels Torgeson, the first summer I was in America (1873). He had a farm in Iowa, near the Minnesota line. While employed there, I worked in the field and had to bind the grain by hand, picking it off the ground and binding it with part of the grain. Then I worked for about five years in the vicinity of Rochester, Minnesota, where I met Ole Brenna, who had a farm rented near Rochester.

On February 8, 1877, I and Ole were united in marriage in a little country church about twelve miles from Rochester, Minnesota. Reverend Torrison performed the ceremony. After the wedding friends and neighbors gathered at the Brenna farm and celebrated, ending with a dance in the evening. This was held in the home.

We lived on this farm near Rochester for sixteen months, and our first child, Henry, was born there.

We heard about land in Dakota Territory and how we could get it by filing a claim and living on it. We decided to try and make a home for ourselves, so we loaded our household goods into a wagon. The father and brother of my husband, Helge and Orjans, accompanied us to Dakota Territory. We had one team of horses, four oxen and eight head of cattle along with us. We got to St. Paul, Minnesota by wagon and loaded an immigrant car there to come as far as Fisher's Landing, as far as the railroad extended (about 14 miles east of Grand Forks). We unloaded our belongings and traveled by wagon to Grand Forks, Dakota Territory.

My husband Ole filed on a homestead and tree claim about four miles from Grand Forks. We rented the upstairs of a building located on South Third Street, owned at that time by the Hudson Bay Company. The Met Theatre would later be located on that site. We lived there for two weeks until my husband with the help of three others completed the building of our home on the homestead. The first part was 12 by 16 feet with a low upstairs. Later in the summer we built on another room. We moved in about the latter part of May 1878.

Ole and Peter Eliason, a neighbor in Brenna Township, decided that they would like to buy the building on South Third Street, where we had lived when we first came to Grand Forks. The men wrote to the Hudson Bay Company and offered $550 for the building and the 100-foot lot. They received a reply stating that the company would take $500, overlooking the $50 which was also offered. This, of course, pleased the two men. The main floor of the building was used for a general store, which was operated by Soulie and Buck. The Brennas and

Mr. Eliason kept the building about two years. They rented the upstairs for an apartment.

I was in Grand Forks once in 1879 and went upstairs to visit. I sat near the window and watched workers drive the piles for the first Great Northern Railway bridge, which was built across the river into Dakota Territory.

After the railroad was laid through Grand Forks, we decided to sell this building. We were afraid it would burn down from the sparks coming out of the train engines. We realized a few hundred dollars profit. Later we were sorry for selling because the lot itself was worth a good sum when the town began to build up.

We built a long sod barn on the farm. We had a well digger from Grand Forks dig a well 20 feet deep. However, it wasn't good water. Someone informed us that if we would dig a well in a low place or sink hole we would get good water. This was done with good results.

I had to make all of the clothing, even the underwear. I also knit the socks and stockings. I did not have a spinning wheel at first, but I did have a Wilson sewing machine which I had brought with me from Minnesota. I sewed a little for the neighbors who spun yarn for me in return.

The first summer, 1878, Ole's father and brother, Helge and Orjans, broke a few acres of land on Orjans' and Ole's homesteads with two teams of oxen and a walking plow. Ole used the team of horses to haul lumber for the other room of the house and for the construction of a barn.

The next year, 1879, they used horses to put in the crop. They had a small seeder and harrow. The first harvester was a hand-binding one. It took three men: one to drive and two to do the binding. They had to work fast, as the grain had to be picked up and tied with part of the grain as it passed through the canvas.

Our farm used to be the stopping place for the settlers from the territory around Northwood. They would leave their homes in the morning and by evening would reach our place, a distance of about 20 miles across the prairie. The next morning they would go into Grand Forks, four miles away. They would do their shopping and return to our farm that same day, in the evening, and stay for another night. In the morning they would start for home. Sometimes quite a few settlers were

**A Gathering of relatives and neighbors at the Ole Lykken farm home,
Milton, North Dakota, 1890**

*A large gathering of people posing for the photographer in front of a log cabin. The cabin
is two stories with a single story addition. It has a pitched sod roof and stovepipe. In the
distance and to one side of the house there is a man with a horse, and another man
standing beside a large boot in the back of a wagon. It was made in 1875 by Markus
Johnson for the North Star Shoe Company of Minneapolis for exhibition at the
Minnesota State Fair. The boot was size 119 and required two steer hides to make. The
boots became the property of Mr. Johnson after the Fair closed. There are approximately
thirty-two people in the photograph.*

there at the same time, so beds would be all over the floor. At times they
would have a jug with them and would get noisy during the night. My
husband, who was a big strong man, would have to come downstairs and
settle the noise.

Squatting Pays Off

Anders Elken

The hardest work I ever had was to fight prairie fires.

Born on November 23, 1868 in Hadeland, Norway, Anders Elken emigrated to America when he was seventeen years old. His family was very poor, and at the age of seven he began working most of the year as a cattle and sheep herder. During periods of time in the winter he attended religious and common schools, graduating grade school when he was fifteen. He was also confirmed in the Lutheran Church that year. For two years he worked as a farm laborer for $3 plus room, board, and clothing per year. He had relatives and friends in the Spring Grove, Minnesota, area. Anders Elken was lured to the New World by letters and reports that described America as the land of opportunity.

I HAD BEEN CONTEMPLATING for some time to emigrate to America, but the drawback was money for passage, which I did not have. So I wrote to an uncle who lived in the Spring Grove vicinity and informed him of my desire. As soon as my uncle learned that I wanted to come to America, he sent me a ticket in the spring of 1885. As there happened to be a rate war on at that time between the different steamship companies, my uncle obtained passage for me from Norway to Spring Grove, Minnesota, for $33.00. I arrived there after an uneventful voyage on the 13th day of June 1885.

After resting and visiting with my uncle a few days, I went to work at a job obtained by my uncle on a farm in the community as a laborer, for which I was to receive $12.00 per month during the summer and $15.00 per month through the fall.

My first impression of the country was not so good. I cannot explain just why I was not so well impressed. It might have been just plain homesickness. However, when I had been here a month or so I began to like it better, and when I received my wages in the fall and was able to pay my uncle in full the money he had advanced for my passage from Norway, I felt satisfied and thought that this was a great country.

During the first three years I was in America, I met people off and on who had been out west in the Dakota Territory, some as far west as Wells County, others only as far as to the Red River Valley. All of them spoke very highly of the country. Those who had been into Wells County told of the government land open for settlement. If a person who was of age had $15.00, he could get a homestead. In fact, at that time a person could get three claims: homestead, tree claim and pre-emption. One did not have to establish residence on a tree claim, but he did have to plant a certain number of trees which had to be alive and cultivated before he could prove up on it. The pre-emption involved establishing residence on the land for a period of at least fourteen months and them paying Uncle Sam $1.25 per acre when one wanted to prove. To homestead one had to establish residence for at least fourteen months, at the end of which you could commute — that is, prove by paying Uncle Sam $1.25 per acre — or you could reside on the quarter and improve it for a period of seven years. Then it was compulsory to prove if you wanted to keep the claim. If a homesteader did not wish to commute he could prove up on it after residing for five years. Then you had to pay Uncle only $15.00, but you had to have at least two witnesses that you lived there. If the proof passed, the government would, in due time, issue a patent to you as owner. The patent is government title to the land.

In the spring of 1888 I decided to go to Wells County. I would not become of age until November 1889, so I could not file on government land of any kind until then, but I had been told that I could squat on land and thereby hold it until I became of age. Of course, that would not prevent anyone else from filing on the claim, but as there was plenty of other land to choose from, there would not be much danger that anyone else would file on it.

I had had steady work since my arrival in America and had saved my money.

An acquaintance of mine, Peter Jonsrud, who had been farming in the Spring Grove vicinity, had decided to quit farming. He obtained employment in a flour mill at Minneapolis, so he was selling his property. I bought from him, in the spring of 1888, two cows, one heifer, and two calves, four- and six-months old. I bought a cast-iron cook stove, cooking utensils, dishes, knives, forks and spoons, and 250 oak fence posts. I also bought a hog, which I butchered, cut up, salted and packed as pork into a barrel. I also bought one hay mower, one corn planter, one corn cultivator, and one breaking plow.

Two friends of mine, Martin and Jon Hagen, also decided to go up to Wells County and get some free government land. They owned property, including horses and oxen. We agreed to share an immigrant car.

During the summer and fall of 1888 I was kept busy assisting my pioneer friends build claim houses. During the winter of 1888-89 I attended school for four months at Timan Quarve's home with Mr. Quarve as teacher.

I squatted on the W½ of the SW¼ of section 4, and the NE¼ of the NE¼ of section 5, and the NW¼ of the NW¼ of section 9, all in township 150, Range 69. In the spring of 1889 I started building a 14- by 16-foot house of lumber on the land, but I was unable to finish it in time to be used the next winter.

In the fall of 1888 I wrote to my parents, who had emigrated to America in 1887 and located in Walsh County near Hoople to come to Wells County. My parents came, but because I had not finished the house, we lived with my neighbor, Erick Hagen and family, through the winter of 1888-89.

Because I would not come of age until November 23, 1889, and because I was afraid I could not hold the claim I had squatted on, I let my stepfather, Ole Lynne, pre-empt on it and occupy the house I had built.

When I came of age, I pre-empted on land in sections 8 and 17, township 150, Range 69. When the time came to make final proof, I found that I would have to pay the government $1.25 per acre for the claim, more money than I possessed. I availed myself of the privilege of changing it to a homestead in 1893. I relinquished back to the government the pre-emption and immediately made homestead entry on 120 acres of the old pre-emption and 40 acres adjoining it, which included a hay meadow.

When the first house was finished enough to be livable in 1889, I and my parents moved in. The lighting was kerosene lamps. There were homemade bedsteads and mattresses. The bedsteads were made of boards and 2x4 studings, the mattresses of ticking filled with straw. We made benches for seats and a table and cupboard of lumber. For cooking and heating we had a cast-iron cook stove. Our summer fuel consisted of prairie chips and hay. We also occasionally used hay during the winter to save on coal and wood. We got some wood and coal at Antelope Lake, on government land, a distance of about 40 miles. I cut and loaded my own wood. I obtained lignite coal in Pony Gulch, near Sheyenne Lake, a distance of 35 miles. I paid ten cents per inch in the wagon box for the coal, but I had to load it myself.

I did my first breaking in the summer of 1888, with only one yoke of oxen — five acres on the claim I had squatted on. I also broke for others for $2.50 per acre. I had only the one yoke until 1891 when I bought a second yoke. In 1893, I disposed of the oxen and bought three horses.

I did not have much time to spend for recreational activities. Hunting wild game birds off and on during the spring and fall of the year was really the only sport I had. During the winters, I spent part of my spare time reading newspapers and light story books, visiting neighbors, and attending an occasional party in the neighborhood. If there happened to be a Fourth of July celebration in the community, I would go there. We celebrated Christmas by attending church and festivities at someone's home before the school houses were built.

Whenever time permitted during the summer, the first couple of years, I would pick buffalo bones and haul them to town where I received $8.00 to $11.00 per ton. This brought some ready cash for incidental expenses — not to spend, for I never spent any money. Every penny I made was used for things I needed.

During the first five years, I lived with my parents most of the time and assisted them in establishing a home and getting their claim broken into fields.

When I pre-empted on my claim, I built a 12- by 12-foot shack of lumber with a slant roof covered with shingles. It had two windows, one door, and a 8- by 8- by 6-foot cellar under the floor. The walls of the shack were covered on the outside with tar felt. I made use of this shack only during the summer months. In the fall of 1896 I decided to make my permanent home. I also built a sod stable large enough to hold my horses and stock. I had put up hay enough for the stock, so I moved what I had not before to the claim in November of that year. I left the work of fixing up the shack for winter's use until I moved in. The old paper on the walls was torn, leaving cracks which let in the cold air. However, before I got started fixing the shack, a Thanksgiving blizzard struck, the worst blizzard I can recall. It lasted for three days. The snow drifted in through the cracks in the walls so that the floor and the bed — in fact, everything in the shack — was covered with snow several inches thick. All I had for heating was a small cast-iron cook stove. It gave just enough heat to melt the snow on the floor around the stove, causing a puddle of water which froze during the night. During the three-day storm I had to wear my cap, goatskin fur coat, and overshoes continually. I could not get to the stable until the third day, and then it took me several hours of shoveling snow before I could gain entrance to care for the stock.

It did not take me long after that to start fixing up the shack so that I would not freeze to death in it. I covered the outside with new tar felt and banked it with snow.

From the fall of 1896 until I married in 1901 I batched, doing my own cooking, dish washing, clothes washing and housekeeping. I stayed and farmed my claim until 1901. In the early part of that year I bid on a 40-acre government script, the SW¼ of the SE¼ of section 5, township 150, Range 69. The government accepted the bid, and I moved my buildings and stock and other belongings onto this tract. I built an addition to my first shack, and I lived in this house until 1905.

On the 18th of March 1901 I married Miss Julia Otelia Gibertson, whom I had known from the time I arrived in America. We became acquainted in Houston County, Minnesota, in the vicinity of Spring Grove where she lived with her parents on the farm where she was raised. Reverend Styrk Reque of the Spring Grove Lutheran Congregation performed the ceremony. Only relatives and a few friends were present at the wedding. In the evening, the parents of the bride gave a wedding dance in their home. After visiting for a short time, we went to our home in Wells County.

My wife contracted tuberculosis of the lungs, and after a lingering illness, she died on her birthday, August 11, 1904 at the age of 28 years. We had one child, Gertie.

The hardest work I ever had was to fight prairie fires. Every fall I had to make fire breaks around my home by breaking two circles around the buildings and hay stacks, about four to five rods apart. After breaking or plowing the circles, I would burn the grass on the space between the circles. By doing this, I could set a back fire when the prairie fire approached. On a windy day or night sparks from a fire would fly through the air and light several rods ahead of the fire, so a back fire had to be set. In addition to fire breaks, I had to keep barrels and rags handy at all times during the prairie fire seasons. When a fire was in sight, I would place the barrels on a stone boat or into a wagon, fill the barrels with water and haul them to where the sparks would light inside the fire breaks. I would soak the rags with the water I had in the barrels and use them to put out the sparks. The first thing I did, however, was to rush out and set a back fire.

I lost many nights of sleep and rest fighting prairie fires. I sometimes went as far as ten miles with neighbors to try to prevent a prairie fire from getting into the community and burning the good buffalo grass that cattle fed on. The prairie fire menace prevailed until the whole area was broken into fields. I even had to make fire breaks around my grain fields and hay meadows to save them from burning.

In 1888-89-90 the crops were light because of the drought. In 1891, however, we all had an excellent crop. Wheat yielded from 20 to 40 bushes per acre, oats 40 to 50, and flax about 15 bushels per acre.

Homesteading in a Jewish Neighborhood near Devils Lake

Louis (Larson) Froguer

North Dakota is the best place in the world to live.

Louis Larson was born on March 28, 1866 in the hamlet of Skein, not far from Norway's capital Christiana (Oslo today). When Louis was only six years old, his mother died, and his father Lars took him to live with an uncle, Hans Larson, in Christiana. Louis attended school until he was ten when he went to work on his uncle's fishing boat. His experience in the Devils Lake region was fairly typical of Norwegian sodbusters — with one exception. Not many Norwegians lived next to a Jewish homestead colony.

I **HAD ALWAYS**, from the time I was old enough to think for myself, wanted to go to America. In 1882 my uncle gave me money enough to add to what I had saved to leave for the United States. I left Norway in July for Stevens Point, Wisconsin. The ocean trip did not mean a great deal to me; I had been out on a boat every day for six years. I traveled steerage. Most of the trip was rough, and nearly all the passengers were ill. I spent most of my time waiting on those who were ill.

The crossing was the easiest part of the trip. When I landed in New York the confusion was so great because the language was one I could not understand and everything was so strange. I felt like sitting down and crying.

I finally got on the train, and at the end of two days reached Stevens Point, Wisconsin. My uncle, Ole Froguer, met me at the train and took me home. I took my uncle's name — Froguer. I worked on my uncle's farm part of the time. At other times I worked for any of the neighbors who might need help.

In 1883 I went to work in a lumber camp near Stevens Point. I worked here all the winters of 1883 and 1884, receiving $15 per month. In the spring I went back to my uncle's farm.

At this time there was so much talk of Dakota Territory and the good land to be had free that I and some other boys who were living with relatives, the same as I was, decided we would go out and see this place. One of these boys, Hans Paulson, had been in Dakota the year before visiting a brother near Valley City.

In 1885 I, Hans and Martin Paulson and Adolph Olson, took only our personal belongings and went directly to Devils Lake. When we arrived, we found the town buried in snow. The houses were completely covered; about all that was visible were the chimneys. The train came in between two walls of snow. The snow didn't thaw until the middle of April. I and the men who were with me stayed in Devils Lake for a couple of days.

Olavious Lundaas came to Devils Lake, and we all went out to his homestead.He came with a sleigh and a team of oxen. There weren't any roads; we just struck off across the country, over the snow banks that were from six to eight feet deep on level, and as hard as rock. We visited at the Lundaas home for a few days and then left for Hans Paulson's homestead. Hans had taken a homestead in the summer of 1884.

Before leaving Devils Lake, we bought supplies, flour, salt, sugar, coffee, beans and matches. Lundaas hauled these over to the shack for us. It was about three miles northeast of the Lundaas' place.

I stayed with Hans until April 20th when I went to work for Christ Hermanson, a farmer not far from the Lundaas farm. I worked for him for one year. I couldn't take out papers to become a citizen until I came of age in 1887.

After March 28, 1887, I went to Devils Lake and took out citizenship papers which I got from T.C. Saunders, the first clerk of court in Ramsey County. I asked Saunders if I should use my own name, Larson, or the name I was known by, Froguer. Saunders said, "It doesn't matter to me what name you use, just so you get the papers in time to vote." The only things he asked me were my name, birth place, and my intentions.

Immediately after getting papers I filed a pre-emption, the NW¼ of section 8 in Cleveland Township. I broke about five acres but did not put in any crop. The remainder of the year I worked for Christ Hermanson in the south end of the township.

At the end of 1888, I did not have the required $200 to have the land made over to me, so I just let it lay. In the spring of 1889 I filed a homestead on the same quarter. I bought a shack from Bennie Greenburg, one of the settlers from the Jewish settlement north of my place.

In 1885 a Jewish company in New York sent a colony of settlers to Dakota Territory to take up land. They settled in the southeast corner of what is now Sullivan Township — a few settled in the northwest corner of what is now Overland Township. The original members of the colony were Dave Slemmerson, Sam Goldberg, Myer Null, Soloman Calaf, Benjamin Greenburg, Phillip Greenburg, and Abraham Adleman. They were good neighbors who took part in all community activities and mixed in politics. In fact, they lived just as any of the early settlers did. They all proved up their land, after which some of them raised money on their land and went back east. Others moved into town and went into business.

Bennie Greenburg moved to Devils Lake after he proved up his land. He lived there until his death. Abraham Ademan also moved to Devils Lake. He and Greenburg went into business together. They bought scrap iron, etc., which they shipped east.

The shack I bought from Greenburg for $10.00 was an 8- by 10-foot tarpapered building. The furnishings went with the shack — a built-in bunk, a small cook stove, a handmade pine table, and four handmade stools.

In the spring of 1890 there was a post office established at Iola, about 20 miles northeast of Devils Lake. The route or trail went directly through my land, and the carrier, Christ Hermanson, went past my shack on each trip. Hermanson made the trip twice a week and received $1.50 per trip. This was discontinued about 1900.

Through 1890 I still used oxen to do all my farm work and to make my trips to Devils Lake for supplies, a distance of approximately ten miles. The trip would take all day. I had broken about five acres and put it all in wheat in the spring of 1889. The five acres I had broken in 1887 I put into oats and barley. The summer was very dry, so the crop was not very good. I got about ten bushels of wheat to the acre. The oats and barley were a little better than that. In the fall of 1889 I broke about ten acres.

In the spring of 1890 I put in approximately 20 acres of wheat. This was another dry year, and the crop yield was about the same as 1889. Through the summer of 1890 I put in all the time I could spare breaking and getting about 45 acres ready to seed in the spring of 1891, when I put in 60 acres of wheat and five acres of oats.

That spring, I tried to make a loan on my land, but I could not get one. The eastern land companies had stopped loaning money on Dakota homesteads. So many settlers had come in, settled on homesteads, and left after proving up and borrowing all they could that these companies were getting too much idle land on their hands. I have been thankful many times that I couldn't make a loan as I might have been tempted to do as the others had done. Eighteen ninety-one was the beginning of my good times. There was plenty of rain, and the crop that year was exceptional.

I started cutting my grain when it was still a little green because I knew it would take a long time to harvest such a heavy stand with oxen. I would start cutting as early in the morning as I could, cut as long as the oxen could stand it, and then I would shock while they were resting. It was very hard to find anyone to thresh for me, but I worked all fall on Christ Hermanson's threshing outfit, getting $4.00 a day for my ox team and myself.

Hermanson started threshing about September 1st, and we moved onto my place about October 20th. It started to rain on the 23rd, and on the 25th it snowed. The snow didn't leave until April. I got only part of my threshing done that fall, so I had to finish it in the spring. The grain I threshed in fall yielded 45 bushels per acre of No. 1 wheat at $1.00 per bushel, but I only threshed about ten acres. The wheat I threshed in the spring — actually June 1892 — yielded fairly well — about 30 bushels per acre. But it was a very poor grade, so I got only 30 cents per bushel for it.

From 1892 on, my crops were always average, until 1900 when the yield started falling off. The average from 1892 to 1900 was about 25 bushels per acre. After 1900 I only got about 15 bushels per acre.

Up until 1902, the settlers north of Devils Lake had to do all their trading in Devils Lake and bring their produce there to market it. In 1901 a company was incorporated in Devils Lake known as the Farmers Grain and Shipping Company. The president of this company was Joe Kelly. He and his brother, Frank Kelly of nearby Cando, and a man named Considine were the members of this company. The purpose was to build a railroad north to the Canadian border.

They sold stock to the farmers, and in 1902 the road was built to Starkweather, 25 miles north of Devils Lake. They ran out of funds at Starkweather and had to stop work. Joe Kelly, the president, after a time was successful in interesting eastern capital in the road and the work was resumed. The work was completed in 1904 at the end of the line, Hansboro, about 95 miles north of Devils Lake.

After the completion of the road, Joe Kelly wrote to the president of the Great Northern asking for an exchange of passes for himself and employees. He wrote back saying he did not see how they could do this as Kelly's line was not as long as the G.N. Kelly wrote a reply saying, "My line may not be as long yours, but it is just as wide." Kelly got his passes.

Making Money and Dancing the Night Away

The Hoiland Family

Our home was a sort of neighborhood center.

In 1848 Aadne and Johanna Hoiland booked passage on a sailboat and headed for America. After a six-week voyage, they landed in New York City and took the train to Chicago. Unlike most Norwegian immigrants, Hoiland was a skilled craftsman, a millwright, and he had no difficulty finding work as a carpenter. In the Rushford, Minnesota area he combined his trade with successful farming. By 1878, when he took up land in Barnes County, south of Valley City, he had a sizable bank account. He paid cash at $2.50 per acre for an entire section (640 acres) and brought with him a full complement of machinery and 32 head of cattle. He also filed on a homestead.

Albert Hoiland, a son born on April 23, 1860, tells his and his family's story. Albert also homesteaded and farmed for several years. After 1904, he went into business selling windmills, automobiles, and other farm-related equipment. He was also an inventor. The Hoiland story is one of success.

FROM NEW YORK, father and mother went to Chicago, Illinois, arriving during the cholera epidemic. Father got a job making coffins. He continued at this during the summer of 1848 until fall, and then, taking mother with him,

45

went to Winona, Minnesota, a boat station on the Mississippi, via the Chicago, Milwaukee and St. Paul Railroad. They lived in Winona from the fall of 1848 until the summer of 1849, and father worked at the carpenter trade when he and mother moved to Decorah, Iowa, where he engaged in the building and contracting business for about one year. During this time their first child, John, was born.

Rushford, Minnesota, on the Ruth River had sprung up as an inland town. The Milwaukee Railroad was building from Winona to Rushford. My folks and son, John, moved from Decorah to Rushford sometime during the summer of 1851 where father continued working at the carpenter trade. The family lived here three or four years, and during this time, two children, Aadne Jr. and Andrew, were born.

In 1852 Mr. Hiram Walker came to Rushford and built a flour mill, and father got a job at his old trade as millwright. Power for operating this mill was derived from the Ruth River. While working in Mr. Walker's mill for three or four years, father bought 40 or 80 acres of land with the money he had saved from his earnings. The land was on Hoiland Prairie, a sparsely-timbered tract of land adjacent to Rushford. Father had the land cleared, built a small house on it, and then sold it. He bought another tract on North Prairie nearer town and built it up.

When the Civil War broke out, father was working at his trade in Mr. Walker's mill when he was drafted. Mr. Walker, not wishing to lose father's services, hired a substitute for $360. This sum was later deducted from father's wages. During this time there were many Indian scares, but none of them amounted to anything in that part of the state. Father lived in Rushford with his family in the winter but moved on his farm in the summer in order to reduce living expenses. He walked to and from his work in Walker's mill in Rushford each day. He sold this land after two or three years and bought 160 acres two miles from Rushford, built it up, and moved his family on it. He did this in order to educate his children better. I was born on this farm. While living there, father continued to work in Mr. Walker's mill in Rushford. He also engaged in farming. As the beer brewing industry flourished at this time, he soon turned his attention to raising hops. He had up to thirty women and girls working for him during hop harvest. This crop was very profitable.

All changes in location made up to this time by my father were prompted by a better opportunity to secure employment, but then he got the western fever. He sold his farm in 1878, and he and my oldest brother, John, came to Barnes County, Dakota Territory. John took a homestead, but father bought a section of land in what would become Greene Township for which he paid $2.50 per acre cash. Then he also took a homestead on the Sheyenne River in section 12 of what is now Oakville Township (Barnes County) in 1878. In 1879 father moved the family from Rushford, Minnesota, and made this homestead his home from then on.

In April 1879, Mother, her mother (Mrs. Ellen Christoffoerson, who had made her home with her daughter's family) and the five youngest children including me, then nine years old, took the train from Rushford, Minnesota, to Valley City. The trip took about one and one-half days. Arriving in Valley City toward evening, we engaged two rooms in Lund's Hotel and stayed overnight. The rooms cost $1.50 each. We also had our meals there. Valley City was young and didn't look like much like a town for buffalo grass was growing in the streets.

James Daily, who in 1878 had taken a homestead on the Sheyenne River (in Oakville Township) 14 miles south of Valley City, came to town to take our group to his home. Mr. Daily had two horses hitched to a lumber wagon on which were two spring seats. This was considered something of a luxury for a settler to own.

There were no bridges over the Sheyenne River then, and Mr. Daily forded the river below the mill dam. From here Mr. Daily struck out across the prairie, for there were no roads or trails. Scouting parties or prospectors who had roamed over the plains in previous years had piled buffalo bones on the top of hills. These piles were from 50 to 100 rods apart. Each pile differed from the others either in size or in its shape as did also the hills where the bones were piled. Thus they served as trail markers for the settlers, who knew where they were and how far they came or where they were going. The trip from Valley City to Daily's homestead required the greater part of the day. When we arrived at the Daily homestead, we children were very sadly disappointed at the appearance of the house. Coming from a well-built, well-kept furnished home to a 12- by 14-foot log house dugout in a side hill along a coulee was a very uninviting change. We stayed at Mr. Daily's place for three weeks.

Our family came to Dakota in three groups or parties: first, father and son, John, came in 1878, bought land took up homesteads and remained during the winter living with Mr. Daily. Second, mother, her mother and the five children came by train in April 1879. We brought wearing apparel with us. Third, the next oldest boys, Aadne Jr. and Andrew, the two oldest daughters, Sarah and Mary, and two hired men left Rushford, Minnesota one week earlier than mother's group. This third party had three covered wagons drawn by oxen. The wagons were loaded with household goods, bedding, furniture, clothes, stove, some farm machinery, and other necessary articles. A crate of chickens was tied on the outside of one of the wagons. They had two saddle horses and drove 32 head of cattle. This party arrived at the Daily homestead three weeks later than the second party. When the whole family was together again, we moved to our homestead and lived in tents and the covered wagons until the house was finished. The third group covered the 500 miles from Rushford, Minnesota, to the Daily homestead in four weeks. Mr. Daily's house had one window in the south besides the door. This door was made of rough boards hung on hinges. It had an iron latch to keep it closed. Upstairs the rafters were within one foot from the floor on the sides and just high enough in the middle so that a person could stand erect. It was not connected with the downstairs but was entered from the outside through a door nearly on a level with the ground.

During the summer of 1879, father built a house and a barn, both of logs. He felled trees in the timber along the Sheyenne and shaped the logs with an axe to fit in the walls of the buildings. The house was 24 by 28 feet, 12 feet high, and had four rooms, a cellar underneath the whole house, and a shingle roof.

Father always provided well for those dependent upon him. In this he had the assistance of a faithful, frugal wife. They always had an abundance of vegetables in season and a goodly store for winter. They made their own butter and cheese — both cottage and full-cream. The curd was made with the aid of a calf's stomach bought in the store at Valley City. They butchered hogs, sheep, and beef; made sausage, cured their own ham and bacon, and dried beef; and rendered the lard and saved the offal which was worked over and made into some article that could be used about the household. Mother and her mother carded wool, spun yarn and knitted stockings, mittens, wristlets, sweaters and caps. The girls made their own dresses and their mother's and grandmother's too, as well as shirts for the men. Material for these garments was bought in a store at Valley City.

Our home was a sort of neighborhood center. Whenever we went to town, we would bring the mail for the entire neighborhood for miles around, and people would come to our place for their mail. In the summer they would get their mail about once a week, but in the winter when the roads were bad and travel difficult, it would be a month or more before the mail would come.

I was too small to do any work on the farm, so I spent the first few years going to school four or five months and then fishing and picking strawberries, June berries, gooseberries, chokecherries, grapes and plums which grew wild in the valley. Some were served fresh on the table while others were preserved for winter use. When I was 12 or 13 years old, I started trapping gophers. LaMoure County paid bounty on gophers, and I went there to trap. In addition to the bounty of 5 cents paid by the county, the local farmers furnished me with room and board. The tail of the gopher was evidence that I had caught it. My earnings from gopher trapping was over $30 in three weeks. At the age of 15 years I started trapping furbearing animals. My catch consisted of muskrats, 34 mink, 4 raccoons, and one otter. The pelt of the otter measured six feet from tip of nose to tip of tail. I received $8 for it. All in all this catch netted me over $100. I bought two suits of clothes. One was my brother John's wedding suit, which cost $35.

Antelope and deer were plentiful in the valley during the fall and winter when the prairie was bare. My father did not allow me to carry a gun. My brothers, John and Aadne Jr., shot many deer and antelope, and the meat was used on the table.

Kerosene lamps were used to light the house. These were augmented with lard lamps and tallow candles, made by mother as follows: lard was placed in metal plates or shallow tin covers. Pure lard or a mixture of lard and tallow was put in these containers, and a wick made of cotton batting, lightly twisted, was laid in the lard. One end of the wick was allowed to hang over the edge of the dish. This end was lighted, and the heat thus generated melted the lard and this kept the lamp alive.

Tallow candles were made from clean pure tallow rendered from the suet taken from the carcass of the beeves which father butchered on the farm for home consumption. Candles could be made in any manner, but mother made hers using the follow apparatus: a frame made of boards one foot deep, 16 inches wide, by three feet long, open at the top and bottom, was laid down open-side up. Wires 20 inches long were laid across this frame, spaced two inches apart. Candle wicks, bought in the store at Valley City, were hung across these wires ten to the wire and then lightly twisted or corded together. A washboiler was placed on the stove and filled half full of water. Enough tallow was added to this to make a coating about three inches thick. This was then heated to liquefy the tallow. Next, one of the wires from which the wicks was suspending was taken off the frame, and the wicks immersed in the tallow and replaced in the frame. All the wires were taken in rotation and treated likewise. This dipping was continued until the candles were the desired thickness. Three-fourths inch thick by one foot long was the preferred size. When the candles were cool and firm, the wicks were cut at the wire, and the candles packed in boxes which were stored in a cool place.

Mother was a frugal woman who made as many of the household necessities in her own home as she could, including soap. Lye for soapmaking came from wood ashes. Ashes from the kitchen stove were carefully saved by storing in empty salt barrels prepared for this purpose: a three-quarter-inch hole was bored in the bottom of each barrel. A plug made from a broom handle longer than the depth of the barrel was inserted in the hole. The barrels were placed on a box a foot high. A three-inch layer of coarse chips was put in the bottom, then a two-inch layer of coarse hay. This made a strainer to prevent ashes from plugging the hole when the plug was removed. When soapmaking time arrived, water was poured in the barrels until the ashes were covered. The ashes were then allowed to leach for a few days. A tripod made from strong poles was set up outdoors. A 30-gallon iron kettle was suspended from this tripod by a strong iron hook. A pail was placed underneath one of the barrels. Then the plug which stuck out at the top of the barrel was raised a little, and the liquid drawn off and poured into the iron kettle. When as much liquid as was necessary was drawn off of the ashes, a fire was started under the iron kettle. The fat, grease and tallow which had accumulated was then added to the liquid in the kettle and allowed to cool to see whether the substance was saponifying. When it made satisfactory soap, the liquid was dipped out of the kettle with a long-handled dipper, poured into shallow pans, allowed to cool, and then cut into bars. These were packed into boxes and put away for future use. Mother made 125 to 150 pounds of soap at one time.

Father made beer for home consumption. Malt for beer brewing was prepared by putting one bushel of barley in a grain sack. The sack was then tied shut, fastened to a rope and submerged in the Sheyenne River and allowed to soak for three days. This soaking so swelled the barley that it made a whole sackful. Clean cloths were now spread on the upstairs' floor when it was warm. The barley was spread on the cloth about three inches thick to sprout. When the sprouts were one inch long, the barley was put in large pans four inches deep. These were then put in the oven to dry the barley quickly. Care had to be taken in drying so that the barley did not burn, which would give a bitter taste to the beer. The dry barley, sprouts and all, was then coarsely ground on a common feedmill in Valley City. A 50-gallon syrup barrel was prepared in the same manner that the salt barrels were prepared for storing and leaching ashes, except that the chips were carefully selected — clean oak — and no hay was necessary. The barrel was filled with round, dry malt. Boiling water was poured on the malt until the barrel was full. It was then allowed to stand for six hours. The liquid was drained off the malt in this barrel and poured into a boiler on the kitchen stove and heated to a boil. Then, enough hops were added to make a three-inch layer in the boiler. It was then boiled for 30 minutes during which the contents were stirred constantly. Then it was strained to removed the hops. The liquid was added to that in the second barrel and brewing yeast was added. When cool, it was put into beer kegs or cider barrels which were left uncorked for three weeks. The beer was then ready to be served. It made a wholesome refreshing drink, especially in the summer, for it corrected the reactionary effect of the river water.

Making Money and Dancing the Night Away

My job with all these home enterprises was to provide fuel and keep fires bright.

Reading material consisted of such books which settlers brought with them from their former homes, including the Bible, prayer books, and hymnals and a few wholesome story books. Since few could read English, the local papers were not very popular. The *Decorah Posten*, a paper published in the Norwegian language in Decorah, Iowa, which carried the news and a good story, was eagerly awaited each week. The subscription price was $1.50 per year.

Dancing was the chief form of recreation. The people danced the folk dances, waltzes, schottisches, polkas, gallop ryewaltzes, and heel-and-toe and square dances. The fiddlers were Carl Abrahamson and John Chapman. The latter also called the square dances. In 1884 a brick schoolhouse was built in Leal Township, but there were no pupils, so it was used as a dance hall.

In 1881 the community Fourth of July celebration was held in Hoiland Park, a somewhat open space in the woods along the Sheyenne River 10 or 12 rods from our home. In the afternoon there was a base-ball game and races. Mr. and Mrs. Pato, whose home was about three miles east of Valley City, was the heaviest couple present. Their combined weight was around 600 pounds. An attorney from Valley City delivered an oration on the Declaration of Independence. Lunch was served by the ladies, and eating began about noon and was kept up until the next morning. Two tables 20 feet long each were set. A platform 50-by 50-feet square served as a dancing pavilion. The crowd started dancing at sundown and kept it up until daylight. Refreshments consisted of several barrels of lemonade, 18 eight-gallon kegs of beer, and several gallons of wine. The beer cost $3 per keg and was paid for by donations. Most men "chipped in" a dollar to pay for the beer, wine, lemons, and sugar. There were no fireworks, but some alcohol was brought along by some people, privately, who wanted something that had a kick. Considering the large crowd and the great quantity of liquor which was consumed, but few people were drunk. The greater portion of the crowd was from Valley City, Leal and Rogers.

In 1889, I, in partnership with my brother, Anton, started farming in Fordensjold Township. We rented the SW¼, section 10. We had ac-

Take your choice the team of oxen? the team of horses?
Two men in a buggy pulled by a team of two oxen, and a man in a buggy pulled by a team of two horses. The scene is on a Park River street, 189-?.

cumulated enough machinery, always buying secondhand machinery and repairing it ourselves. I owned three old horses and Anton owned three two-year-old steers and one bull the same age. He broke these when they were only one year old. Anton could do more work with his two yoke of cattle than I could with my three horses. We two brothers "batched it" until June 1897, when I got married. Anton married about six weeks later, and we dissolved our partnership in the fall of 1897. I continued to farm for seven more years.

I quit farming in 1904 and moved to Nome, North Dakota to engage in the windmill business. In connection with this I carried pumps, pipes, tanks and feed grinders. From 1908 to 1911 I handled the EMF automobile, and in 1911 I added the Hudson-Essex to my line. It was at this time that I invented the radiator shutter known as the Hudson-Essex shutter. In 1912 I invented the Hoiland Wild Oat Separator. I rented out my home in Nome and moved to Fargo in February 1915. In 1916 I invented a smut-treating machine. The same year I bought the lot at 1221 Front Street, Fargo.

Trading Iowa for Northern Dakota

Mikkel Hylden

"Go west, young man," seemed to be the watchword.

On April 12, 1865 Ole and Anna Hylden and six of their seven children set sail from Bergen, Norway for the United States. Son David remained at Ulvik on the tiny family farm. Three years later David sold the farm and joined his family in Iowa. Mikkel Hylden lived on his parents' St. Ansgar, Iowa farm and worked as a hired man until 1873. Born on February 19, 1847, Mikkel Hylden had earned enough money to buy a quarter in Mitchell County, Iowa. He batched it on his farm for four years. In 1877 he married Brita Torblaa. By the time the Hyldens left for Dakota, they had three children: Anna, Tina, and Ole. Like many Dakota land seekers, the Hyldens had a good farm in a good place. They wanted a better farm in a better place.

At this time there was a movement toward the west. "Go west, young man" seemed to be the watchword. The call of the western prairies also came to us, and it was music to our ears. Like so many others, we decided to cast our lot with those who had gone before and who had sent word back of the wonderful opportunities that awaited those who had courage and backbone to face the difficulties that always present themselves to the pioneers. Little did we realize what lay before us — what struggles, what temptations, what discomforts, what hardships. We were ready to face the future, not only its difficulties, but what we envisioned would be a time when the prairies would be dotted with homes of a peaceful and liberty-loving people. We looked forward to communities where we could meet and together enjoy the friendly spirit that characterizes the liberty-loving Vikings.

With these thoughts uppermost, we made preparations to move from Iowa. We rented out our farm to a German named Miller. Located at Northwood, Iowa was a man by the name of Edmund Wambeim who came there from Lodi, Wisconsin. He was employed in a wagon shop, and when he heard that I had decided to move to Dakota Territory, he at once decided to accompany us.

We began to prepare to leave in earnest. We packed our household goods and hauled them to St. Ansgar and loaded them on an immigrant car. Besides the household goods, I had one team of work horses, one team of three-year-old colts, one yearling colt, a cow and a calf. Mr. Wambeim and I have been close personal friends and neighbors ever since.

We decided that I was to travel in real style by accompanying the horses and cattle in the immigrant car while the others, consisting of Mr. and Mrs. Wambeim and their daughter Mathilda, my wife and our three children were to take the passenger train. We did so during the late days of March 1881.

I arrived safe and well at Grand Forks, which at that time was the terminal of the Great Northern Railroad, on Saturday, April 2, 1881. I found that the others had arrived just one day ahead of me. As soon as we had unloaded our car we set about to load as much as possible on the wagon and sleigh we brought along. What we did not have room for we stored. We proceeded on our trip to Grafton. The weather was fine, and we made good progress even though we had the colt, the two cows and the calf tied behind the wagon and sleigh. However, after having traveled some distance, the calf decided this was too much of a good thing, so he decided to lie down in the snow and refuse to take another step or even get up. The calf won and was placed on the sleigh where he kept the women and children company. The first day we proceeded as far as a little town by the name of Christiana located north of Grand Forks. Here we stopped overnight, and the next day we arrived at the home of Lars Torblaa which was our destination for the time being. This farm was six and one-half miles southwest of Grafton. Here we tired travelers found a hearty welcome and rested for a few days. I and Mr. Wambeim then set out to look for land. We traveled up toward Hoople then westward past Garfield and finally entered the heart of Golden Valley, where we decided to locate and build our homes, plant trees, build roads, the schools, and last, but not least, a place of worship.

Returning to Grafton, Mr. Torblaa offered to take us to Grand Forks in order to get the rest of our property, but by the time we arrived in Minto his team was all tired out owing to the condition of the roads, so he was forced to return home. I and Mr. Wambeim then had to proceed on foot. Just south of Minto, we met a man driving a team and wagon. With him and his wife was a little boy sitting in the bottom of the wagon box. The man stopped his team, and after exchanging greetings informed us his name was Frazier. I'm quite certain that the little boy sitting in that wagon was none other than Lynn J. Frazier, would become governor and U.S. senator.

From Minto to Grand Forks we had a very pleasant journey. It was spring time when a young man's thoughts are turned to love, and love the Red River Valley we did. In this superlative mood we trudged along the road covered with slush and waded almost to our hips in crossing streams formed by the melting snow. We finally reached Grand Forks and lost no time in making preparations to transport our belongings to their destination. Along the banks of the Red River there was an abundance of timber, so we set about felling trees and cutting the trunks into logs of proper length. These we fastened together with ropes into a raft measuring 8- by 16-feet. We began to carry the boxes, trunks, kitchenware, etc. onto the raft and had almost completed the task when, "Lo and behold," the raft began to sink. What to do? We grabbed the first box or trunk within reach and headed for solid footing and saved the situation just in time. After a hurried consultation, we again set to work felling trees and building a raft of the same size as the first one. We securely fastened the logs together and once more loaded our cargo and were ready for the journey down the river. It was Sunday afternoon about four o'clock that the work was finished, and it seemed that practically the entire population of Grand Forks was on hand to witness our daring adventure. The plan was to push out from land and give the raft a test before we set out on the long trip. The majority of the people proclaimed us a couple of fools and predicted failure; the minority were a trifle more optimistic and said we might reach our destination safely if we were careful and had good luck. After a little trial of our raft, we felt satisfied that everything was O.K., so we decided to come ashore to provide ourselves with food for the trip. But try as we would, we were unable to get to shore and finally we were caught by the swift current of the river and carried downstream. This was at a time the river was running its swiftest from being fed by streams and rivers by the melting snow. There was nothing for us to do but float on, drift on toward our goal. Soon, however, eventide was creeping over the land, and we began to lay plans for anchoring safely in a harbor and waiting for a new morn to come with its bright and shining light. At a bend in the river our raft floated quite close to the shore, and we managed to reach some branches of overhanging trees and thus pull the raft to the shore where we tied it fast to some trees. We dared not venture out on the river at night because steamboats were sailing up and down. After landing we began looking around for a place to sleep. Luck was with us, for we spied a little cabin in the woods. We found it unoccupied, so we made ourselves right at home and went to bed expecting to enjoy a good night's sleep and to wake up refreshed and ready for another day's travel. But, to our surprise, we received the unwelcome company in the form of swarms of mosquitoes bent on taking unfair advantage of us. Well, the upshot of the whole matter was that we had to take turns smoking the pipe of peace in order to keep the pests quiet and likewise take turns catching a few winks of sleep. Thus we passed a peaceful and quiet night that will linger in our memory. The next morning we were on our journey bright and early and made splendid headway. The only incident worthy of mention was that a steamboat was coming up the river. This put fear into our hearts as the boat was sending out waves that surely would capsize our raft. But, to all good luck, the steamboat pulled up to the Dakota side of the river to replenish its supply of wood and gave us a chance to pass safely.

Arriving at Acton on Tuesday afternoon, we finished our trip down the Red River. The cargo was carried ashore, the raft taken apart, and everything covered up until we could get rigs to haul it to its destination. After completing our task, we set out to find something to eat. Entering the hotel, we asked for food and were given a little coffee, some bread and milk. What did this amount to for a couple of husky, hungry fellows? We rattled the dishes for more, but the waiter politely informed us that it was all they had. We got up to leave when the bartender told us that we would have to settle for the meal. We said we would pay when a meal was given to us, but the bartender promptly locked the door and informed us that we would not leave until we paid him 25 cents a piece. We had no alternative, so we paid and departed, flat broke as we headed westward for the Lars Torblaa home. However, by this time it was getting dusk, and as the country was new to us, we decided it would not be safe to travel at night. Seeing a house in the distance, we headed for it hoping to find a place to sleep and maybe something to eat, as we were almost famished. When we arrived at the house of the new settler and asked for something to eat, we were given bread and some sour milk. When we finished, Mr. Wambeim began a conversation with the new settler while I quietly worked my way toward the door. I reached the door knob just at the moment Mr. Wambeim asked the settler how much we owed. Neither of us had a penny. "Well," said the new settler, "I think it ought to be worth 25 cents." Just as he finished I flung open and door and said, "Many thanks for the meal," and headed right for the wide open spaces with Mr. Wambeim close at my heels. We did not dare to look for a place to sleep until we were at a safe distance from the new settler's, but we at last felt we were safe and settled down for the night in a straw pile. The next day we arrived at Torblaa's where we were given all we wanted to eat and we rested for a day. After that, I made several trips to Acton before getting all my goods moved. Mr. Wambeim hired a man and team to haul his goods.

The next move was to the valley where we began to cut down trees and haul them to the place that was to be our future home. At this time the township was not surveyed or named, but Golden Township just north was surveyed. I was unaware that there was a correction line between the two townships, so my guess about the boundaries of my land was not very exact. I selected a site for my house about where I thought the northeast corner of the quarter would be. However, when the township was surveyed in August 1881, I found that I had built my house in the center of the quarter. In building our houses, Mr. Wambeim felled the trees. I hauled the logs, and Nels Monsebraaten and Iver Strand-satern helped us build. I and Mr. Wambeim settled in Golden Valley during the last days of April 1881.

Then I began breaking the prairies. During the first summer I broke 30 acres before I learned to my dismay when the township was surveyed that I had started in or about the center of my quarter and plowed halfway in on the quarter south of mine. As the prairie soil was not fit for raising a crop the first year it was plowed, I set about to find some place to plant potatoes and a garden. I planted our gardens over a mile southwest of my home. There was timber, and Mr. Wambeim grubbed out the trees and I did the plowing.

An Indian trail leading from Walhalla to St. Paul crossed my quarter just on the west side of my buildings. There was also an another trail that led from the Turtle Mountains and joined the main trail at some point north of my farm. The ruts in the trail were so deep that it was difficult to cross it with a wagon. Here and there I found evidence scattered over the farm that Indians had roamed the valley.

The year 1882 was in many respects a very important one for me. I put in my first crop of wheat that year on the 30 acres I broke the previous year. There was also an election held to determine whether the county seat would be located in Grafton or Minto. When the returns came in, Grafton came out victorious. This same year the first township election was held, and I was elected to the first board of supervisors.

In the fall of 1882 I harvested and threshed my first crop of wheat with horse power. I also hauled the first load of wheat to Grafton. I would start out in the morning before sunrise, drive to Grafton, sell the grain, stay overnight, and drive back home the next day. The round trip was about 50 miles.

During these early days, religious services were held at the homes of settlers, but later on when a schoolhouse was built at Grafton, services were held there. On Christmas morning we got up and did the chores, dressed up and drove seven miles to services. We arrived on time.

Seven Years was Enough on the Homestead near Haynes

Louise Woodwick La Mont

I was so homesick, I couldn't even cry.

They stayed on the land near Haynes in southwestern North Dakota just seven years. Dusty La Mont was only three months old when his parents immigrated from France to Montreal, Canada in 1880. Louise Woodwick was born that same year in Frost, Minnesota to Louis and Christen Woodwick, Norwegian immigrants. Around 1900 the two met in Blue Earth, Minnesota, and not long after decided to join the thousands of new land seekers of the Second Boom. Adams County was just opening up as they arrived in 1905. Louise and Dusty had a tough time making it in a country of marginal rainfall. They worked hard, but work wasn't enough. Lack of rain drove them off the land. In 1912 they returned to Minnesota.

WE LANDED OUT ON OUR HOMESTEAD, about fifty miles south of Richardton and thirty-five miles from Mott, North Dakota, on November 3, 1905. We traveled cross-country the 25 miles from Richardton. We had our team, a dog, and just a few pieces of furniture.

We built a sod house — just a small one, first. We then sent for our furniture, but it went past Richardton, so we did not get it for three months. I had to cook on a heater; and, believe me, I had a hard time!

There was hardly standing room in our little house after we put our cook stove and bed in it. I made cupboards out of the boxes I got groceries in. I hemmed flour sacks to make curtains for the cupboards and for the windows in our shack.

We were on our homestead just two weeks when we had the worst blizzard in years, November 14-16, 1905. We had a barn built of sod for our horses, and our shack was completed — such as it was. So we didn't suffer very much, except for the lonesomeness. Our neighbor, Mr. Clyde Bobb, a rancher who lived a mile from us, lost a lot of sheep. He came to our shack during the awful storm and asked my husband to go with him to find them. We hated to say, "No," so my husband went; he was gone for three days. I didn't expect them to get back in that storm in such a wilderness, but they finally came. They found some of the sheep several miles away. Some they never found at all.

I was alone three days, but the worst of the situation was forgotten in the excitement over Mr. Bobb's sheep. I had hardly anything to eat! We had come out to the claim with some people by the name of Van Eschen, and we left what food we had at their house until we could get our shack built. Consequently, we had little to eat. No bread! I tried to make pancakes with only flour, water and lard — that's what the dog and I lived on for three days.

I was so homesick I couldn't even cry. The first year was the worst. After that, people started to coming looking for land, and the Milwaukee Railroad came in. My husband freighted lumber and many other things from Richardton to what became Haynes. Those trips took a week or more with horses. I was so lonesome and homesick; I stayed alone all the time. It was surely trying. Coyotes would howl around our shack at night and scare me nearly to death.

We started to farm and had a couple of good crops. Then the weather got so dry — it wouldn't rain. We had a good crop in 1908, I recall. All the other years we were there the crops were poor. We sold our homestead, bought another, and built a good house, but it was too dry. We sold our place to a man from our old home, Fred Willett.

We had to fight lots of prairie fires. In October 1906, we were out all one day and one night fighting fire to save our home and our neighbor's.

My husband and I went out to North Dakota first. Two years later his married sister and brother came out. They homesteaded five miles east of us.

We went over to a hill to obtain native lime to plaster our sod house. We also sent for some wall paper for our shack — it surely looked nice. We also had a floor in our shack while most of the homesteaders had only dirt floors.

When we first came, we got our mail at Mott, North Dakota, thirty-five miles distant. My sister-in-law and her little daughter burned to death at McHenry, North Dakota, and I didn't get the message or letter until three weeks after she was buried. I surely felt badly over that, but we were there on the homestead; we made up our minds we would stick it out.

I got sick out there once. I found out afterward, when I got to Rochester, Minnesota, that I had suffered from appendicitis. Our neighbor, Pete Oyen, who lived three miles away, said there was doctor near Cedar Creek, about 20 miles distant. He started for him on skis. There was lots of snow at that time, and he was gone for two days. He returned with some medicine. I improved some, but did not really get well, so I went back to my folks at St. Paul and then to Rochester where I had an operation.

From Shepherd Boy in Norway to Governor in North Dakota

Ragnvold A. Nestos

Not a word of English could I speak or understand.

Born in Voss, a mountain region about 70 miles east of Bergen, on April 12, 1877, Ragnvold A. Nestos was the eldest of ten children in the family of Andres and Herborg Nestaas. Because the Nestaas farm was located in a sparsely populated mountain region, Nestos' schooling was sporadic and usually not more than three months a year. As a youth he was in charge of herding the cattle during the summer months. His family was devoutly Lutheran and held family devotions twice daily. Nestos homesteaded but worked the land just enough to gain title. His interests turned to law and politics. He never married.

I CAME TO THE UNITED STATES at the age of 16 in 1893. I had reached a grade about equivalent to the fifth in American schools, and not a word of English could I speak or understand. The journey across the sea, on money borrowed from my uncle, E.R. Nestos of Buxton, North Dakota, was made by way of England and

Fourth of July celebration at Inkster, North Dakota, 1894
Long line of horse drawn wagons and carriages on street. In one wagon is a band. Another wagon has U.S. flags on corners and on each horse. People gathered on boardwalks.

the trip over the Atlantic on *The Prince*, a small boat of the American Line. It took 13 days from Liverpool to Philadelphia. When I landed there, I had but 85 cents in cash, but I had brought along from home a lunch of hard tack and butter, enough to last until I reached Buxton. At Philadelphia I found that the butter container had been smashed, and my only good suit of clothes thoroughly buttered, but the hard tack was still intact. I came to Buxton on June 4, 1893 with little or no work to be had because the President Grover Cleveland hard times had started. The Fourth of July was celebrated in that little town that year, but I had a lone nickel with which to celebrate the day. From the middle of July I worked long hours in haying for 75 cents a day, harvesting at $1.25, and threshing, $1.25 to $1.50 to pay my uncle for my ticket, to get clothes, and to get ready for school. I did some of my farm work July through September for Budd Reeve, the well-known sage of Buxton.

In November 1893, I started in the first grade in the Buxton public schools. I worked for my board, doing chores during the week and working in my uncle's harness shop on Saturdays. Because of a lack of discipline and other unfortunate circumstances in school, I made very little progress the first year. But in 1896-97, Professor Irving McDonald came as superintendent of the school. He took a great interest in me. I worked hard to make progress, and his extra help and encouragement made that progress possible.

I first experienced public speaking in the debating society of that school, and I still remember the glow of pleasure and pride when, after a rather halting participation in the debate, Professor McDonald took me aside and told me that if I would but persist, he felt sure that some day I would do well as a public speaker.

At the close of the threshing season in the fall of 1895, I grew restless, and, incited by the stories told by the threshers who spent winters in the lumber woods, I forsook school and went with some companions to Eau Claire, Wisconsin. I spent a couple of months in the lumber camps near Hawkins, and when I took sick, I left for Minneapolis to work as such odd jobs as could be secured. In January 1896, I went back to Buxton and entered school, and in April 1897 took the teacher's examination and taught a term of school near by. On the advice of the county superintendent, I studied orthography and other subjects at the Mayville Normal. After one term there and teaching two more terms, I went back and completed the course at the Normal in two years, graduating in June 1900.

The president of the Normal School was Joseph Carhart, who had previously been the teacher of English and oratory at De Pauw University for 13 years. He had counted among his pupils and ardent admirers such men as former Senator Albert J. Beveridge; attorney James R. Wikerson of Chicago, later a United States district judge; Roy West of Illinois; Professor A.W. Moore of the University of Chicago; Senator Watson of Indiana; as well as others. As a teacher in psychology, philosophy, and logic, and in knowledge of men, he was the greatest inspirational force that came into my life, as he was in the lives of so many others, including the galaxy that came from his classroom in De Pauw.

I was joined by three others in having to work my way through school: Dr. E. Vinje (of Chicago), H. Haldorrson (in the Customs Service at Sherwood, North Dakota), and B.O. Skrivseth (an educator). We four rented rooms and prepared our own meals and took care of our own quarters during the whole of that school year. We took turns in the preparation of food and in doing housework. At the end of the year, we determined that the average cost to each of us was $2.00 per week.

During the summer, I did farm work, bookkeeping, clerking and canvassing. In the meantime, I had filed on a homestead in Pierce County, where I spent the summer of 1900. After making final proof that fall, I enrolled at the University of Wisconsin for a college course. I did most of my work under Professors Richard T. Ely, M.V. O'Shea, and Julius Olson.

At Wisconsin, I founded a new literary society, the Olympia, and took an active interest in debating. I graduated in 1902. During the school year, I earned a share of my way by waiting on tables, collecting and delivering laundry, and doing other odd jobs. During the summer I added some more to my experience as a canvasser, going out in charge of a squad of seven other student canvassers, selling a book in southern Wisconsin and northern Illinois.

The next fall, I entered Law School at the University of North Dakota after a summer spent in canvassing, clerking and bookkeeping. During that year, I entered more extensively into public debating, representing the Law School against one of the university societies, and later representing the University in a debate against the Unversity of South Dakota at Vermillion where my team was victorious in debating government ownership of railroads.

On the evening of the debate, President Garret Droppers of the University, who presided, announced a victory for South Dakota by the vote of two to one. This result stood through the evening reception, at which the North Dakota debaters were the recipients of the profuse sympathy of the university people and of compliments upon the splendid debate put up and the fine spirit shown under the sting of defeat, the justice of which might easily be questioned. But the next morning, accidentally, the truth was discovered and the correct result — a victory for North Dakota — finally, though belatedly, was announced.

From May to September of that summer, I toured England, France, Belgium, Germany, Denmark, and Sweden with Otto B. Dahle of Mt. Horeb, Wisconsin, a classmate. I then spent a couple of months visiting my parents in my childhood home in Norway and with my mother at a chalet in the mountains. In the spring of 1904 I graduated from the Law School of the University of North Dakota and started a law practice at Minot in partnership with C.A. Johnson, who was the Republican nominee for governor in 1906 and 1908.

During my Minot residency, I was interested in political and civic affairs generally. In the fall of 1910, I was elected to the legislature and served in the session of 1911 as the chairman of the Committee on Taxation. That winter the House of Representatives voted to impeach one of the district judges. A board of managers was elected to try the impeachment proceedings before the Senate; I was one of the five. The trial was conducted before the Senate in Bismarck during April and May 1911.

In the fall of 1912, I was elected State's Attorney and served in that office from 1913 to 1916. I was a believer in and a supporter of the state prohibition law; and as a prosecutor, was active in law enforcement. I was a member of the state and national bar associations, and for a couple of years a member of the Committee on Grievances and Disbarment of the state association.

In 1916 I became a candidate for the Republican nomination for United States senator. In a field of four, I ran second. Porter J. McCumber, who had been Senator for 18 years, was re-nominated by a small majority.

Prior to 1910, I was actively interested in library work and was a member of the library board of Minot after 1905. I helped to bring the Carnegie Library to Minot and to make it a real asset to the community. I was also president of the State Library Association for three years and ex officio member of the State Library Commission.

I have been on the state executive committee of the Y.M.C.A. and of the state Sunday School Association for many years. I am a member of the Lutheran Church and have been superintendent of one of the largest Sunday schools of that denomination for a period of 12 years as well as being a Bible class teacher. I am a member of the National Board of Education of the Home Missions Committee for the North Dakota District of the Lutheran Church.

In the spring of 1920, I was a candidate for the endorsement of the independent forces for governor of the state, but I was defeated at the Minot convention by William Langer, who had deserted and turned on the Non-Partisan League. I was out in the campaign and made a large number of speeches for Mr. Langer and, in every way, promoted his candidacy. Shortly after the close of the campaign, I made a trip to Norway to visit my mother who had been very sick. I had not seen her for 17 years, so I spent a month with her in the mountains of Norway. I desired to get back for the campaign that fall to support J.F.T. O'Connor, who then had the support of the Independent Voters' Association for the governorship. Finding that there was no chance to get passage from Norway on either first or second class until after the election, and anxious to help O'Connor in the campaign, I decided once more to make the trip across the Atlantic by steerage, as I had done in 1893. I landed in New York on the *Mauritania* September 25th and came back to North Dakota immediately and participated actively in the campaign to elect O'Connor.

A delegate convention of the Independent Voters' Association met March 30-31, 1921 in the city of Devils Lake. Every county was represented; the total membership was nearly 600. The convention was called to consider whether any of the officials inaugurated in January should be recalled. After nearly two days of debate, we decided to recall the Governor, the Attorney General, and the Commissioner of Agriculture and Labor. I was selected by unanimous vote to make the race for the governorship against the man who then occupied the office, Lynn J. Frazier.

A long and bitter campaign followed, and on October 28, 1921, the election resulted in victory of the Independent candidates. I won by a majority of 4,102. On November 23, 1921, the newly elected officials were inaugurated, the first to be elected in a recall election.

In June 1922, I secured the Republican nomination for governor in North Dakota by a majority of 11,066, and at the general election in November 1922, I was reelected by a majority of 29,273 to a term expiring January 6, 1925.

After I closed my second term as governor in January 1925, I made a Chautauqua lecture tour for the Redpath organization through some 80 of the leading cities of the ten southeastern states, speaking on "The Responsibilities of Leadership."

Before Railroad and Towns: The Earliest of Norwegian Settlers

Andrew and Hanna Paulson

They had to swim the rivers and walk the entire way.

Andrew Paulson, who was born on April 8, 1843, migrated from Norway to the Eau Claire, Wisconsin area in 1866. Hanna Bröken at age four accompanied her parents from Norway to Potter County, Pennsylvania in 1852. The Brökens farmed there for eleven years prior to moving to western Wisconsin. There Andrew met Hanna, and they were married in 1869. They lived in Chippewa Falls where Andrew was employed in logging. In 1871 he lost all his money and property in a bad business deal. That is where the story of these two very early Red River settlers begins. The story is told by their daughter, Jennie, who was born on the Richland County farm in 1876. Jennie married a Canadian-born teacher, William Baisley, in 1897. William, who had filed on a homestead southwest of Wahpeton in Elma Township, spent winters until 1905 teaching in one-room township schools. Jennie and William reared seven children on the homestead.

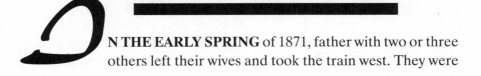

N THE EARLY SPRING of 1871, father with two or three others left their wives and took the train west. They were headed for Fort Abercrombie. The train traveled as far west as Benson, Minnesota. They decided to walk the remainder of the way to the fort. They had to swim the rivers and walk the entire way. They arrived in the last of May or first of June 1871.

Father was hired as a veterinary surgeon at the fort and also did some blacksmithing and horse training. He wrote to my mother and told her of the conditions at the fort and suggested that she be contented to live there alone in Wisconsin until there were more improvements in the West. But after she got the letter, she decided that if he could live there, she could also; so she packed up her few belongings and with her baby, she took the train west. The railroad was not completed to the fort; so, when she reached the end of the line, the trainmen told her she would have to get off, if she hadn't changed her mind and return to the East to wait until the train service was better. She laughed at them and said she would get to the fort even if she had to walk all the rest of the way. She talked to some of the people in the little town where the railroad ended, and she learned that there was a construction crew going out to the fort in the morning, but they wouldn't take her because they did not have a place for her to ride. She went to the tracks in the morning and begged to be taken along. After she convinced the men that she and the baby could sit on top of one of the construction cars, they allowed her to go to the fort with them. It was in November, and she lost the baby's warm shoe while she was on the car. The baby was good, but they both got very cold riding in the open.

She arrived in the last of November in a snow storm. She was the first white woman to come to the fort by train. Regular service didn't start until the summer of the next year, 1872.

In the spring of 1872 mother and father left the fort with a wagon and team borrowed from the fort along with a tent for the trip. They located on section 14, the SW¼ of the NE¼. The Wild Rice River crossed through their forty acres and supplied them with water, and the timber growing on the banks was used for fuel. Mother spent most of the first summer alone because father was on the trail to and from Fort Abercrombie or Fargo, where he did the shipping. He had to haul the lumber for their home from Fargo, and he got his mail from the fort. There were many days during which mother was alone at her home in the tent, and on one of these days when father wasn't going to be home for the night, she had a visitor who asked to be fed and given shelter for the night. This visitor was an old Indian woman. Mother told her that she could stay in her tent if she wanted to and that she could eat with her if she desired. Mother set the table, and the woman sat down to eat. She drew a large knife from under her shawl and began to cut the vegetables which had been set before her. Mother was very frightened but tried not to show her fear. The Indian ate and then prepared to sleep. Mother didn't sleep much that night. In the early morning the woman left, thanking mother for her kindness. About noon of that day two men on horseback rode up and inquired about any travelers who had passed by. Mother told them no one had passed. Then they told her that they were looking for an Indian woman who had married a white man some years previous. He had been sent to jail, and while he was in jail she had been running around and had had a baby. When she learned that her husband was going to be freed, she killed her baby and ran away. She didn't want her white husband to learn of her actions while he was in jail. The men were looking for her as she had committed murder and would have to go to jail.

None of the Indians or other travelers who passed by the tent ever harmed her. There were many traveling by because they followed the river. Once she was frightened by an Indian man who came to her home and just looked around and then turned and left. She grabbed the baby and ran for the woods, and the two of them stayed there until she was sure that the Indian didn't intend to return. Father arrived home late that night, but the Indian didn't return nor take anything when he was there.

While mother lived near the river, she continued to make soap for the fort. She liked to do it, and it meant more money for her to use to keep house.

That fall father built a small two-room house. He had the first frame building in the area. He could afford only enough lumber to build one room so he had to add one log room. The logs were taken from the grove on the river bank. The house had two windows and one door. It was furnished with the most simple of furniture. The first winter they had just two chairs and one high chair for the baby. A table and springs were set up on the ends of the logs. The next few years they were able to get, and later were able to make, more furniture. Father made a couple of three-legged stools. He carved them from wood gotten from the grove — being handy with a knife, he was able to carve lovely stools.

The first winter there were no neighbors near enough to be of assistance. There were a few newcomers, but they had settled on the prairie north and east of them. The next two or three years brought many more to the township, and in 1875 the settlers decided they needed a school so the folks gave up one of their rooms to be used as a school room. The teacher lived with them while he taught the classes. The term of school was from one to four months in the good weather. Those settlers, who had room to keep the teacher and have the school in their home, did so.

About 1878 the settlers decided to build a school, and John Hagen gave a small spot of land free to be used as the school grounds. The settlers gave all the time they could to build a schoolhouse. It was roughly made, but served the purpose. The children sat upon benches made from planks or half logs smoothed on one side and set upon blocks of wood. This school was used for many years. I remember going to this school and recall how the older boys and some of the girls went to the river to swim during the noon hour or at recess.

In 1878 the hoppers were so bad that they ate the outside layer from the fence posts. The settlers had to cut hay and pile it up in small piles around the fields. When the hoppers settled in the hay, the settlers started the piles afire and tried to burn the hoppers.

Father was the first settler to have horses on the farm. He had lovely horses, and he even sold many to the farmers. But more often, he loaned them to the neighbors to use to finish their work. He trained horses and did a great deal of horse trading, buying and selling. He spent a great deal of time with his horses, grooming them and keeping them looking nice. In 1878 he bought a binder. He was the first farmer in the locality to own one. This binder used wire instead of twine.

My parents were proud of the fact that they were living in America, and they believed that they should teach their children the English language as well as their native tongue. Father succeeded in getting the settlers to send their children to the public school during the time it was open and sending them to religious and Norwegian school when the other school was closed. But he realized that the young people would most likely live in America, and they would need to be educated in the American way if they were to be successful.

Father moved the family north to the prairie in the first house on section 12. It was a five-room, one-story building with a floor space of 16 by 28 feet. It had seven windows and two doors. Father built a new house which had six rooms in 1893.

I married William Baisley on June 26, 1897 in Wahpeton. We were married by Reverend J. Studinicka. We came south into Elma Township where William had a small shack on his homestead. We lived the first summer in the shack while we were building a larger house. Our new home was a four-room house — two downstairs and two upstairs. It was furnished with the nicest furniture William could buy at the time. He had several head of cattle and horses with which he made our living on the farm the first year.

We had five boys and two girls. William came to North Dakota in 1890 from Canada where he had lived with his parents. In 1891 he filed on the homestead in September. As a single man, he taught school in Richland and other counties. He had been a teacher in Canada before he came to Dakota. He was a farmer of activity who realized the growing necessity of modern improvements. He was very active in getting the petitions started for and carrying through on bringing the telephone south to his farm, thus serving many others. He also fought for mail service to reach as far south as his farm, which is near the state line.

After filing on the homestead in 1892, William began looking for work as a teacher. In the early spring of 1893 he was offered the unfinished term in the J. Shea School in Elma Township. He taught there that fall and in the same school in Eagle Township in 1894 and 1895. In the fall of 1896 to March 1897 he taught in Summet Township; from March 1897 to 1898 he taught in Belford Township. He remained at home with me and our children from 1898 to 1901. He had rented most of the land while teaching, but I and the children lived there. He returned to teaching in 1901 in Hart Township in South Dakota. In the fall of 1902 he was hired as teacher in Greendale Township. He gave up teaching in 1903 and remained at home with his family until 1922 when he accepted a school position in Logan County. In 1924-25 he taught in Emmons County.

He was elected to the office of township clerk in 1900 and served the township until 1912. He was assessor from 1918 to 1922. In 1923 he was elected justice of the peace. He was school clerk from 1912 to 1918. In 1905 he got up a petition to bring mail service south to his farm, in 1907 a petition to get the phone line south. He was the U.S. Census enumerator for the 1920 and 1930 Census in Elma Township.

My husband remembers a blizzard in 1897 when he was teaching at Summet. I and my brothers and sisters happened to be visiting at the same home where he taught near Abercrombie. We young people spent the afternoon and a night visiting. Then it began to snow and blow. It kept up for three days. Then it seemed to clear up, so William left the farm and headed south to Wahpeton. He had a horse and cutter and followed the railroad tracks all the way. The snow was so hard and so packed that he didn't know if he was on the right of way, but he did know that he had found a hard path to follow, which was a blessing, because if he had gotten onto the soft trail he would have been lost in the storm. He finally arrived in Wahpeton. Here most of the streets were covered with great banks of snow, and the folks had tunneled through the drifts. The tops of the two-storied buildings could be seen from the tops of the drifts, but not one-story buildings, which were completely covered with snow. The same was true of the town of Abercrombie. Here, too, people tunneled through the streets. No lives were lost in this storm that William can remember.

Just east of Murray Post, a small town on section 23, was a shack which had been a "Blind Pig." In 1902 two boys were coming from town when a storm came up. They were lost, but they found this building and got inside and built a fire. The storm had blown the chimney from the outside, and when the boys, Henry Hankie and Julius Ziebroth, built their fire, they built such a big fire that the roof caught on fire, and they were burned to death. Their horses were also burned. One of the team got away from the fire and reached home with the harness still burning on its back. It died as well. Several years later people saw two white horses appear on the road ahead of them and then disappear when the

Ole Myrvik wedding, Milton, North Dakota, 1894
Large group of men, women and children outside log cabin, with snow on ground.
Bride and groom in front center.

travelers got up to them. Several settlers swear that they have seen this ghost team.

An Indian by name of Garle married a white girl named Annie. Annie had reared two children, the oldest six, the baby about two. One morning she got up after her husband. While he was in the pasture getting the cattle in, she started getting breakfast. But as she went to light the fire, it exploded and she caught on fire. She managed to get the children out of the house. Then, when she tried to put out the fire which was burning her, it was too late. She was badly burned, and she died from those burns.

In 1900 we Baisleys were invited to a wedding. Mr. and Mrs. Portner were to be married. William went, but I remained at home. The celebration after the wedding went on for two days and two nights, until the beer was gone. Then the guests left for home. The folks drank and ate. The music was furnished by a band from South Dakota. My husband can't remember the names of the members of the band. There were only four of them.

There were many dances in the homes in the 1890s and early 1900s. After the settlers began to build barns, we had barn dances to which everyone in the locality was asked to come.

Homesteading near Ambrose during the Second Boom

Ole E. Sims

The country was desolate and dreary.

Of the four children of Henry and Engborg Seims, who farmed in Hardanger, Norway, only one son migrated to America — Ole. "Smitten with wander lust," to use his words, he arrived in the United States at age twenty during 1884. He first came to northern Dakota as a railroad worker when the Great Northern was pushing its tracks from Minot to Williston. Ole, who had shortened his name to Sims, went on to Marysville, Montana, where he was employed a a miner for fifteen years. In 1903 he returned to North Dakota where he homesteaded in what was to become Divide County. The second boom was in full swing as thousands of new homesteaders claimed the last land in northwestern North Dakota. He started farming at a good time: excellent crops and high prices.

AFTER ARRIVING IN AMERICA, I worked as a farm hand in Iowa. I received eighteen dollars a month for my services. That was pretty good pay, because you could buy a good pair of overalls for sixty-five cents and other things in proportion. Gradually working westward, I was living in Minneapolis, Minnesota, in the spring of 1887 when the Great Northern Railway decided to extend its line west from Minot. When I heard about it, I joined a work train and arrived in Minot, Dakota Territory, in April 1887.

My first impression of the territory was anything but favorable. As the construction gang worked westward from Minot, the men remarked time and again that "Jim Hill is sure going to go broke now!" The country was desolate and dreary and appeared unfit for civilization.

Buffalo bones covered the ground at White Earth, so named because the ground was white with bones. I believe that the government's theory was that the Indians had to be driven out in order to make room for the white people and that the best way to do so was to starve them. The buffalo were stampeded into the flats, and the soldiers shot them down by thousands and thousands.

When the construction crew arrived at Williston, there was just a shack and saloon there. The first sight we beheld was a bunch of drunks sleeping in the sun. Occasionally one would stagger to his feet and reel into the saloon for another drink. Then he would stagger out and drop down along the side of the building to sleep some more. The conditions were simply awful. It made a profound impression on me because I had always been in dry states. I had never seen anything like it.

From Williston westward, the only white people we saw besides the other members of the crew were at Fort Buford and at an Indian agency at Poplar, Montana. The road was built from Minot to Great Falls, Montana in four months. It was a gigantic undertaking at the time. The grading was done with wheel scrapers pulled by horses and mules. These scrapers held a yard of dirt; it took two men to hold a scraper while it was being filled. I drove four mules on one of those scrapers for $1.50 a day plus board. This was pretty good pay, and there was no chance to spend any of it.

I estimate that there were over ten thousand men on the crews. Camp was moved about every three weeks. At times, when we were finishing a section, we could see the smoke of the train approaching over the new track behind us.

One camp, near the Dakota line, was near a large gulch where the Indians had a large encampment. The men used to go over and watch the Indians. One evening, they had just killed some animal and were preparing to butcher it when we arrived. One squaw took a front leg and another a hind leg of an animal they held over the fire until all the hair was burned off. Then they cut the carcass open and took out the entrails and placed them in a large kettle over the fire to cook — without washing or cooking them in any way. As the evening was chilly, I stepped close to the fire and spread my hands to warm them. One of the squaws jumped at me swinging a big, long knife. I hastily retreated. She must have thought that I wanted some of that "stuff." The women then proceeded to put up the animal much as a butcher would slaughter a pig or cow. After the meat was cut up, it was washed by a squaw taking a mouthful of water and spraying it on a piece of meat. She scrubbed the meat as she did so. Then the meat was ready to be cooked.

The Indians were peaceful; we experienced no trouble. At a point about two miles west of Williston, near the border of the Buford Reservation at the time, the soldiers refused to allow us to proceed for two days. So the crew lay idle while the railroad and government officials ironed out differences. Then permission came from Washington, and the work went on.

In the fall when the road was completed, I went to work in the mines at Marysville, Montana, where I lived for fifteen years. In 1889, I became a citizen of the United States. At that time I changed my name from the original Seims to Sims. I wanted a name I didn't have to spell every time I told it to someone. On July 25, 1896, I married Miss Lena Henning at Helena, Montana. Five children were born to us at our home in Marysville and one at our new home in Blooming Prairie in Divide County in North Dakota.

I had returned to North Dakota in 1903 to file blind on the southwest quarter of section 19 in township 163, range 98. Then I drove up and looked at my land to see what I had got. Deciding it was a good piece of land, I hired Hans Hougland, a neighboring homesteader, to build me a shack and to plow fire breaks. I then got a leave of absence from my homestead and returned to Marysville for the winter.

In the spring of 1904, I returned to my claim, arriving just a few days before my leave expired, and found it almost all covered with water. I learned that there were floods in the spring in this country, and all sloughs and hollows were filled with water. Quite a few settlers abandoned their claims in disgust. I would have left, too, if I had not already invested so much money. I decided to make the best of the matter.

I had planned in advance for settling that spring. I had ordered a new kitchen range and a table and chairs sent to Ray, North Dakota — also a wagon. This equipment was hauled overland to the homestead. Mrs. Sims and the children arrived that summer. I borrowed a team from my neighbor, Mr. Ole Thorson, and drove to Portal, North Dakota to meet them and haul them home. During the summer we sodded up the shack for warmth and put up a few outbuildings.

We secured provisions from Old Crosby, a town located just across the line in the adjoining township east. This was about a mile west of the present site of Crosby. Here Mr. S.S. Nelson operated a general store. Dr. Lancaster had an office here, and a man named Herring ran a hotel.

In the spring of 1906 I planted my first crop, a five-acre field of flax. The Soo Line built its railroad out from Flaxton, cutting across the township. It terminated a mile west of the township, and the town of Ambrose was established.

During the summer, I decided a school was necessary for the children. I interested some of the neighbors, and we held a meeting at the home of Rud Anderson. On June 5, 1906 we organized the school district. Oscar Storhein, Rud Anderson and I were elected directors, H.H. Lohmeyer was elected treasurer. A. Ryan and H.K. Hougland acted as judges of the election. Rud Anderson and I were clerks along with Mrs. Rud Anderson.

The board secured the services of Miss Martha Berg to teach school and arranged to have a building constructed on the southeast quarter of section 8. There was quite a little controversy over the location of the school house, and it was later moved to a point a mile north, where some of the patrons always wanted it. School opened about September 20 but was discontinued during the winter months. It then ran late into the following summer.

That summer of 1906 we also took care of our religious needs: the Lutheran congregation was organized with Martin Monson, Peter Helland, Hans Hougland, Andrew Ryan, Halvor Rue, Carl Ebbeson, Sven Sussag and I serving as the original members. The first services were held in the Soo depot in Ambrose with Reverend Hjelmland of Columbus, North Dakota conducting. After that, services were held for some time in Miller's Hall, an old opera house on the second floor of A.

Miller and Son hardware store in Ambrose. In 1912, a fine modern church was erected in the southeastern part of town.

In the fall of 1906 I harvested my flax with a mower and threshed out 90 bushels. I marketed the crop at Imperial, North Dakota for 85 or 86 cents a bushel. They told me I was getting a pretty good price.

The spring of 1907 was one of abundant moisture. On the 17th day of May I was plowing with three oxen and two horses on a gang plow and had been going around a big snow bank on the side of a hill. Late in the day I decided to try and plow through below the bank and got stuck in the mud. The plow sank until it was almost out of sight, and the horses floundered around in the mud until they lost their footing and fell down, but the oxen calmly laid down and went to sleep. It was a tedious task to untangle the animals and get them out.

Our daughter, Florence Lillian, was born on November 28, 1908 at our home, but she passed away in October of the following year. Sorrow again visited our home in 1914 when our youngest son, Arthur, was called to his eternal rest.

In 1908 we organized the township, and I was elected one of the supervisors. By this time business had increased in the northern part of the county. People found it very inconvenient to be so far from the county seat at Williston. There was much agitation for dividing the county. On November 8, 1910, the matter was placed before the people, and they voted overwhelmingly to divide the county between townships 159 and 160, with the only opposition coming from a few townships along the line of division. Blooming Prairie was one of ten precincts voting solidly in favor. Divide County became a reality.

There was much speculation about the location of the county seat. Noonan and Ambrose were considered the favorites, but their political maneuvering went wrong, and Crosby was designated until the people voted on a permanent county seat in 1912. The people of Ambrose and Crosby waged a furious campaign. On election day, a severe blizzard raged all day, so a very light vote was cast. As a result, Crosby retained the county seat.

A tornado accompanied by a high wind swept through the county on August 15, 1911. It did considerable damage and took a few lives. The tornado itself passed a little to the south of our farmstead, but the

***Andy and Mandus Hultstrand plowing with the
Pioneer tractor Fairdale, North Dakota, July 10, 1912***
*A Pioneer tractor with an 8-bottom plow plowing a stubble field.
Large pieces of wood are attached to the rims of the wheels, perhaps used to attach
additional outer wheels. One man is driving the tractor and the other is standing on the
platform of the plow, operating the controls.*

wind did considerable damage on the place. My boys were sleeping in a
granary when the storm struck. When the roof blew off, the boys started
to climb out over the walls. I tried to call to them to stay in the protection of the walls because the air was filled with flying lumber and wreck-
age, but they could not hear me. When a stack of hay started to blow
into the building, they ran for safer cover.

In 1914, I decided that we had outgrown the homestead shacks. I
built up a fine new farmstead.

In response to the demand for more wheat brought on by the war in
Europe, I purchased a large tractor and plow outfit in 1916 from the
Oil-Pull company, which delivered it with no down payment. I agreed
with the company to make one payment in the fall and the balance the
year following. I made the first payment as agreed, leaving a balance of
$3,500. I decided it would be a good idea to pay off the outfit in full, so I
asked the bank to loan me the money, even though I already owed them

about the same amount. The banker was glad to do so. Now I owed the bank about $7,000. I paid off Oil-Pull. When I offered the bank a mortgage on the tractor outfit to secure the loan, the banker told me that my note was all that was necessary.

About 1910 the American Society of Equity was organizing around the area, and farmers were quite enthusiastic about a cooperative of some sort. Some farmers organized an Equity hardware store in Ambrose, and I was prevailed upon to buy a share. Although I was not very impressed with the venture, I finally bought some stock and later was elected to the board of supervisors. When the new board to which I was elected took over, we found the store in a deplorable condition financially. Many thousands of dollars worth of merchandise had been sold on credit and could not be collected. We called for a members' assessment of $100, but this was just a drop in the bucket. So I and some of my neighbors put in $1,000 each, but that too went, and the store eventually failed. We lost all of our investment.

I was also a member of the Ambrose Farmers Elevator, which I have always staunchly supported and which I served several terms as a member of the board of directors.

A severe hail storm swept through the country in the fall of 1920, just before harvest time. It ruined the crops. I and my son, Oscar, were home alone at the time. It kept us busy nailing blankets over the windows where the hail broke the panes. This storm was so severe it gouged holes in the siding of our home.

We experienced our first serious drought in 1931 when the crop was a total failure. It was the first time in the history of our community that the land produced nothing at all.

On the Banks of the Knife River

The Hans Siverts

Quite a land boom was on just then.

Not many Norwegians homesteaded in the ranch country of Dunn County. In the spring of 1886, however, Hans Siverts left Norway and headed for Dakota Territory. He put together 320 acres through homesteading and tree claiming on the banks of the Knife River. That fall his wife and three children joined him in what would become their lifelong home. Hans started out like most homesteaders; he grew wheat for the market and oats for the horses. Over the years, however, the Siverts developed their farm into a successful dairy operation — an aspect of farming usually associated with German immigrants. Hans' wife tells her family's story.

I CAME TO DAKOTA TERRITORY from Norway with our three small children. My husband had immigrated early in the spring to find us a home. When I arrived, Dakota was just enjoying the most wonderful Indian summer, so warm and beautiful in its wonderful attire of gold, brown and red. Our summer in Norway had been so cold and rainy, so it was quite a change. My husband had decided to settle down out north of the Knife River. Quite a land boom was on just then. He located a homestead and also filed a tree claim. From Minnesota he took an immigrant car containing a team, cow, young stock, farm implements, lumber, household articles, grain of different kinds, and chickens. Soon the cellar was dug and the shack built. When I left New York for the West, I was certain that my ticket included the baggage, but when I arrived in St. Paul, I learned I had to pay extra for it the rest of my journey. I did not believe this was true, so when the agent came and asked if I would pay or leave the baggage a few minutes before we left, I answered, "The baggage can stand." I came to my destination with our three small children — nothing more.

I suppose most have seen a sailor's traveling bag. It is made of heavy canvas and is round all over; some are long, some short. Such a one was included in my baggage, but it was of unusually big dimensions. When the depot agent saw this, he said, "There comes a Norwegian torpedo." The torpedo had just been invented about this time, and my monstrous bag resembled one. This one, however, proved to be a great blessing because it contained good, warm, winter clothes and bed clothes of every description, which surely were needed when winter came with snow and cold.

Our shack had only single board walls lined inside with tar paper. It was here we lived through the terrible winter storms. It seemed to me it was one blizzard after the other with deep snow. The stove stood red hot, and some bad days we kept the children in bed to keep them warm. The shack was well banked up, and we had a good supply of coal, but it was cold anyway. When the door was opened and the hot and cold air would mix, it was nearly impossible to see anything in the room, but my husband made a little entry of the torpedo, which was a great help. We never liked to have cats and dogs in the room, but I remember that first Christmas evening. The snow fell steady, and the storm howled around the corners, so we invited the dog in — a happy dog! We had two neighbors, one living two, the other four miles away. We did not see each other very often in the winter months. It was a long, lonesome winter, but we enjoyed it the best we could, and we escaped any sickness. My husband had his horses and stock to take care of, and the three children kept me busy. Surely there were no luxuries in that little home — homemade table and benches — but it was our lot as pioneers, and we bore it bravely.

After the winter, the following summer months had plenty of hot and dry weather. Oh, what a desert-like wind and heat we had those first summers! When spring came, my husband started his breaking of a field, but his implements were few and very primitive. Forty acres were

The Hans Siverts

broke and seeded by hand: how his arm ached when he came home!
Only some oats and wheat were cut and hauled home for the horses and
chickens. We harvested nothing else those first years. The summers
were very hot and dry.

We lived on the homestead for about a year before the first minister
visited. We called him to come baptize the first-born child in our family
here in Dakota. We were glad for his visit. Our only means of transpor-
tation was the lumber wagon, so it was not any joy ride. My husband
rumbled along in it, but I preferred to stay home. When he did not have
too much work at home, my husband hired out to earn some money,
which we badly needed. The children and I did not like to be left alone,
but we had to stand it. One time when he left he told me to watch the
milk cow and not let her cross the rising river. I watched her, but before
I knew, she was over on the other side. The only thing I could do was to
leave the children and wade that high river. When I reached the other
side, my clothes started to freeze up. I looked like a lady with one of
those old crinolines on. The cow got home, but she was very cold.

Frequently we had visits from Indians. They traded in Dickinson at
that time, and their road was only a few miles from our house. Certainly
they liked to see the newly arrived white man's home. They came alone
and in groups and liked to be helped with a little coffee, sugar, matches,
and bread. Once there came a bunch of them — men, women and children — just as a rain storm came up. I was alone with the children and
had only this little room, but the rain came with force, so I had to invite
them in for shelter. Opposite the entrance, on the wall, we had a little
white marble statue of Christ, and I noticed that one of the Indians
bowed his head when he saw it. If I had known that a missionary had
been working among them for ten years, I would never have been afraid
of them. Quietly they came, quietly they went, and they never harmed
us in any way. In the years gone by I have learned, and my personal belief is, that the Indians are of good stuff. There never would have been
any war between the red and the white man if the white man had been
fair in all his dealings with the red man.

In 1889 Dakota territory was divided into North and South Dakota.
North Dakota's first governor stood high in our estimation. Once
someone brought into his office a satchel containing $100,000.00. A

85

voice said, "This money is yours, Governor, if you will allow the Louisiana Lottery a home in our state." The $100,000.00 and the Louisiana Lottery rot. Our newborn state could go in among the other states pure and free. And we, the citizens, knew that in our governor's chair was a MAN.

Year by year our family increased, and the shack proved to be too small, so we built on. Our stock increased also little by little. We took in stock for herding, so my husband could stay at home and work. He was an unusually industrious man. He built a stable for the milk cows of the heaviest logs I have seen and had stanchions for 25 cows. It was a wonder to see how every cow could go into its own stanchion without a single mistake. The milking of all these cows was quite a process, but there were many good and willing hands. We made a great quantity of butter of excellent quality, but the price was low those years.

Soon the children were of school age, but there was no school for them to attend. The territory around our homestead was unorganized. We had to hire a private teacher and pay her from our own meager income. We had been free from any sickness until then, but the first teacher brought the measles into our home. We continued with private teachers for a few years. Then my husband and a neighbor got together and took their rights as American citizens in their own hands. With the law on their side, they organized two school districts, built school houses, and hired teachers. All went well until the wealthy cattlemen protested the taxes, which they said were too high. The land fell back into an unorganized state of affairs again, and our prospering school history ended. We poor settlers had to go back to private teachers once again. The first one we hired after the schools closed brought another kind of measles. Nearly the whole family took sick. We had a little Sunday school, and every day I had time, the children and I studied Luther's catechism and Bible history. All of our children have been baptized and confirmed in Luther's faith.

Index

Index

First Ladies Aid of Highland Church, Nekoma, N.D.
Back row: Mrs. Richard Heard, Mrs. Lars Erickson, Mrs. Ole Gjevre,
Olava Amundrud, Mrs. John Amundrud.
Front row: Mrs. Edward Erickson, Mrs. K.W. Haugen, Mrs. Knute Gronhovd, Mrs.
Anton Amundrud, Mrs. A.B. Flom, Randine Bakken

About the editors . . .

Historian D. Jerome Tweton returned to his hometown, Grand Forks, North Dakota, to teach in the University of North Dakota history department in 1965 after receiving his Ph.D. from the University of Oklahoma. For most of his thirty-year tenure at the University, he served as department chairman. Tweton's books include The Marquis de Morès: Dakota Capitalist, French Nationalist *and* The New Deal at the Grassroots: Programs for the People in Otter Tail County, Minnesota. *A senior consultant to the North Dakota state partner of the National Endowment for the Humanities, Tweton has written and edited books and articles about the history of North Dakota for citizens of all ages, including text books and instructional material for classroom use. In addition to his work as an academic historian who has edited publications, written seven books and scores of articles, Tweton has participated in over 300 public humanities programs in North Dakota and throughout the nation. He and his wife Paula own and operate a bed-and-breakfast in a renovated turn-of-the-century home which is on the National Register of Historic Places, the Beiseker Mansion in Fessenden, North Dakota.*

Everett C. Albers has served as the executive director of The North Dakota Humanities Council, the state partner of the National Endowment for the Humanities, since it began in 1973. Albers is one of the founders of the modern Chautauqua movement which features first-person characterizations of historical writers and thinkers presented in tents during summer tours of the Great Plains. He holds an M.A. in English from Colorado State University and has taught humanities and English. A North Dakota native who grew up on a family homestead in Oliver County, Albers lives with his wife Leslie in Bismarck. They are the parents of Albert and Gretchen. Albers operates Otto Design, a desktop publishing concern, as an avocation. He co-edited The Legacy of North Dakota Country Schools *and the 1998* Behold Our New Century: Early 20th Century Visions of America. *He has written several children's coloring books featuring Seaman, the dog who went with Lewis and Clark.*